GONE
TO THE DOGS

GONE
TO THE DOGS

Business, canines and a passion for
chasing dreams. One woman's
journey.

Helen Morphew

DEDICATION

To Rob and El Gingero

Contents

"We who choose to surround ourselves
with lives even more temporary than our
own, live within a fragile circle;
easily and often breached.
Unable to accept its awful gaps,
we would still live no other way.
We cherish memory as the only
certain immortality, never fully
understanding the necessary plan."

– Irving Townsend

PART 1

The journey begins

Family selfie

Breaking the news

I stood quietly by the open French doors, my heartbeat sounding loud in my ears. They hadn't noticed me yet, so I waited, feeling bubbling excitement and a smattering of apprehension – was I really going to voice this mad idea out loud? Asha, our energetic Pointer cross rescue dog, was the first to sense I was home and her tail thumping on the wooden floor alerted the others to my presence. My husband Rob jumped up from the sofa and came towards me, "Hey babe, how was your morning?" he asked as he leaned in to give me a kiss. A chorus of "Hi, hi darling" followed from my mum and friend, Claire, who were both visiting from the UK and enjoying a late morning tea on the sofa while they caught up on all our news.

"I need to tell you all something," I told them.

"You might want to sit back down for this," I said to Rob as Asha wriggled around by my knees with a toy in her mouth. I gave her a bit of a fuss and then walked to the centre of the room and looked with trepidation at three expectant faces.

It was a Saturday lunchtime and I had just returned from one of my regular volunteer shifts at the local animal shelter, something I do every month which usually involves picking up vast amounts of dog poo, and a lot of cleaning, sweating and laughing, dog walking and cuddles. I absolutely love and look forward to this every month. However, this morning had given me a revelation. Today someone new joined the roster to massage some of the dogs, and our supervisor asked whether anyone would be willing to help her. After much elbow poking, sideways glances at my fellow volunteers and comments such as "dog massage?!" I volunteered. I thought, why not I'll probably never see anyone massage a dog again.

And that experience was to change my life.

Now here I was, back at home about to make a big announcement. So, I took a deep breath...

"I want to be a dog massage therapist," I said quickly. "I want to do this for a living." Then I held my breath, looking around the room at three very dear confused and surprised faces. "Don't say anything yet, let me explain." I sat down and told them about the morning, how the therapist was introduced, my volunteering, the young anxious and jumpy dog the therapist had chosen to work on, the dog who was more interested in playing with the other dogs than human attention. My job had been to minimise any outside disruption by holding up a bed sheet around the dog's bed area, and of course I was able to see what was going on. To my complete surprise the previously hyperactive dog had completely relaxed. So much so that when the therapist had finished working on her, the dog had crawled into her lap and promptly fallen asleep. It was truly amazing, and I knew right then and there that it was something I wanted to do. What if I could make a career out of this?

Rob was the first to say something. "Well. I did not expect you to say that," he said. "I didn't even know there was such a thing as massaging dogs." One of the many things I love about my husband is that while he may well have thought I was completely and utterly bonkers, he is always supportive.

My friend Claire was clearly trying not to laugh and chose the moment to focus on her teacup.

My mother, on the other hand, seemed quite speechless.

"I know it sounds really nuts and I obviously need to do my research," I said. "But you know that I've always wanted to work with dogs, and this is something that really excites me."

Finally, Mum spoke. "Well obviously yes you need to do your research darling, but it actually sounds wonderful." Mum had been a physiotherapist before she retired so she understood the physical benefits of massage.

Capturing my gaze, Rob said encouragingly, "Go for it babe, I'll back you."

And that's how it started.

That's the moment I turned my back on the business world I had been a part of for 15 years and started a new career as a canine massage therapist.

Don't get me wrong, I had really enjoyed my career as a human resources manager, but I was just feeling kind of over it. Before Rob and I had emigrated to New Zealand from the UK I had worked for many large organisations in London and I had loved the challenge of working with senior managers in fast-paced environments. Since moving to New Zealand and settling in Auckland, I had been lucky to work with similarly great companies. What was increasingly true though, was the passion I had felt for my business career had faded, and my craving for something more purposeful had grown.

A deep desire of mine was to be able to one day work with dogs, and it was a colleague who had first suggested that if I volunteered at the shelter that might satisfy my desire. Sadly, the opposite was true, and the more time I spent in my volunteer role, the less I felt fulfilled by business life. Sitting behind a desk for most of the day, and working frequently on a computer, I had shocking posture and was a regular client of the in-house massage therapist who would calmly and methodically chip away at my neck and shoulder tension. Massage for dogs made perfect sense to me, and I started to think about my own lively dog and wondering whether she got headaches and muscle knots from running around the park after her frisbee.

I organised lunch with Jody who was our vet to get her thoughts about my intended career change. We'd become firm friends at puppy obedience classes when both our dogs had been small, and then it turned out she was also our vet.

I was feeling a bit anxious when we met up because I was unsure what Jody would say and I knew I would need the support of at least one vet before I headed down this path.

Me: So, I've been thinking about a bit of a change of career.

Jody: Oh yes? What are you thinking?

Me: I'm thinking about working with dogs.

Jody: Great, doing what?

Me: Well you know when you have an injury or you're a bit sore and you go for a massage and it makes you feel SO much better?

Jody: God no, I've never had a massage, can't bear the thought of someone touching me.

Me: Oh. Right. Well. Um. Right well, I'm thinking of doing dog massage.

Jody: Couldn't you do doga? I do yoga and I saw that on YouTube recently, that would be really cool.

Me: Stop it! Be serious.

Jody: I know, I'm joking, tell me more...

So, I did. And by the end of our lunch she was a lot more clued up on the benefits of massage and supportive of me working on some of her clients once I was qualified. She also suggested I meet with the owner of the practice to talk to him about it too. I felt such relief with this first proper conversation done, and a lot happier and positive that what I was about to embark on could work.

I spent the next few months doing research, spending hours on my laptop surfing the internet for insights on canine massage. I managed to track down the person who had been my initial inspiration and after making contact with her it boosted my resolve that this was definitely something I wanted to do. It was important for me to talk to her, to find out more about what it was actually like to massage dogs, and her passion was infectious. Sadly, being such a new discipline, there was nowhere in New Zealand where I could study, but through my searches I found a reputable course in Chicago that really interested me, The Chicago School of Canine Massage. It seemed to have a good balance of practical and theory and offered an intensive course which I knew would suit my learning style. The first stage involved a phone interview which I was nervous about – what if they didn't accept me? – as I had no real background in either massage or dogs really. But the phone interview went extremely well and after I'd filled in a short form (explaining why I wanted to do this, my expectations of the course and any previous canine experience) and sent it off I was accepted, and my enrolment was confirmed. Break out the champagne!

As the course didn't start for a few months I enrolled in a long-distance learning course on canine behaviour and care. My poor old brain... having to do assignments again was a challenge after years with no study, but it helped to get my brain back into the right mode, and six months from that initial encounter and 'lightbulb moment', I was on a plane to Chicago to start my canine massage adventure.

On my way

As I started getting ready for my trip to Chicago the enormity of what I was doing started to dawn on me. I have always enjoyed travelling, even brief work trips where really all you would see was the inside of a hotel room and glimpses of a city from the windows of a cab as you were bundled from airport terminal to office. But this was different. I was going to be away on my own for a month, doing something that to be perfectly honest still seemed a bit crazy.

When I was looking into where I could study, I chose what I considered the very best course available. If I was going to change my career after so many years then I had better make it count and go to the best institution possible – I thought of it like my very own Oxford or Harvard for dog massage! I needed the course to provide me with the level of education that would set me up to work alongside veterinary and canine professionals. I wanted a good understanding of both theory and practical hands-on learning, and this course looked like it would do both far better than any other I could find.

I'd never been to Chicago, and I would be lying if I didn't say I felt excited about the opportunity to adventure in this big city. When I caught up with my dad and told him where I was going, he had no end of facts and figures about how Chicago was one of the most dangerous cities in the world and gun crime was a serious issue. As any dutiful daughter would, I soothed his fears and concerns by telling him how careful I would be (and reminding him that I used to live in London), but I also made a mental note to stay very safe and noted down any 'problem' neighbourhoods that I shouldn't inadvertently stray into. The truth though is I was more concerned about temperature and whether my New Zealand winter wardrobe would be any match for the legendary Chicago wind.

I was going to be away from home for a month and I hadn't been away on my own for a couple of years, so it was feeling a little scary.

The day of departure had started very unusually for me. I had misread my flight time and was ready for an 11.55am departure which was seven hours too early, which meant I was uncharacteristically organised and had more hours than I needed to feed my nerves. Ever since I was a child going on school trips I have been plagued by crippling anxiety when I travel alone so the extra time wasn't ideal, but I knew that once I was on the plane it would all be ok. Rob drove me to the airport and as is tradition in our family, we shared a glass of bubbles in the bar before I went through passport control.

Me: Oh my gosh I feel so nervous now.

Rob: It's normal to be nervous but don't be, you'll be absolutely fine.

Me: But what if it all goes wrong and this is a huge mistake?

Rob: It won't be, you are going to love it.

Me: I'm going to miss you and Asha.

Rob: I know. I'll send you photos of her though and we will Skype each other. Seriously, I know you're going to have a great time.

Me: Yeah. I know. I'm just freaking out because it's actually happening.

Rob: You know there really is nothing to be worried about. You love flying so that'll be great and before you know it, you'll be starting class and hanging out with dogs. You'll be in heaven.

Me: You know me too well!

With that we said our farewells and I was on my way.

Once I was on the plane, I felt more settled, and the 12-hour flight from Auckland to Los Angeles was good, but with long delays on connecting flights it was past midnight before I arrived at my rather uninspiring looking accommodation in Chicago. I felt completely exhausted, jetlagged, and really wasn't too sure what day or time it was... and on top of that I was more than a little in shock that I was actually there.

To say my motel room was horrible would be an understatement. It was situated on the ground floor with huge windows looking out to the carpark at the rear of the building which freaked me out, and the interior couldn't have looked more unattractive. I felt tired, nervous, anxious and more than a little overwrought as I Skyped Rob and burst into tears. The build-up to the trip and the enormity of what I was doing finally hit me full on. Rob was so calm and gentle, and I finally calmed down and fell asleep.

The next morning, I was woken by a serenade of car alarms from the carpark and as I opened my eyes the nerves from the night before returned with a lurch. Feeling a bit sick I grabbed a quick shower, got dressed and headed down to reception to find out how to get into Chicago and start my explorations. It had been dark when I arrived, so I was desperate to get my bearings. It was the weekend, and while I vaguely knew where I was in relation to downtown Chicago from my google surfing, I was excited to get out and about and do things.

The taxi driver who picked me up was a star. I'd forgotten how big the cars were in the United States compared to New Zealand and he drove speedily along while I slid from side to side in the enormous back seat, keeping up a constant chatter the whole way to the train station.

"I love your accent; you must be English," he told me. "What brings you to Chicago?"

"I'm going to the Chicago School of Canine Massage," I proudly announced and then waited – over the last few months I had learnt that I needed to let that sink in before I expected anything more.

One evening in Auckland a couple of months before, Rob and I had been in a bar with friends and I was chatting to a guy I hadn't seen for a while. He asked a completely normal and previously uneventful question "So, how's work?"

"Oh, I've had a bit of a change of direction since I last saw you."

"Oh yes, where are you working now?"

"I'm going to be working for myself."

"Consulting?"

"Not exactly, dog massage. I'm going to Chicago next week for a course in canine massage therapy."

A shocked disbelieving look "What?????"

"Yep, dog massage, cool isn't it."

"Oh. My. God. Are you serious? I thought you were winding me up. What on earth is that about?"

And that was pretty much how it went with almost everyone I spoke to. Thankfully most were not as scathing as this particular encounter but nonetheless I had gone from telling people I worked in human resources which normally acted like a conversation stopper (or the start of a giant whinge about their manager, employee or their own human resources department), to dog massage which elicited laughter, scorn, incredulity and comments about candles and whale music.

My taxi driver however simply nodded and then moved on to tell me about the local pizza joints I should visit. In reality, I thought, dog massage probably wasn't the most unusual thing he would have to deal with that day!

He gave me detailed instructions of what I should do and then dropped me at the train station where I did the second part of my trip to get to the heart of Chicago. Just looking at the scenery as it flashed past the train window fascinated me. The architecture, the colours, the road layouts, everything! I was in a new place and I loved it. I caught the subway a short distance and finally on foot wandered through the streets looking for Topshop and H&M (it's a bit of a compulsion I have whenever I get to a big city as there was no Topshop or H&M in Auckland at that time). Along the way I spotted a gorgeous looking bistro with people sitting at tables on the sidewalk enjoying the autumn sunlight and I made a mental note to go back there once I'd finished my shopping.

First on my list was a new coat. As I had suspected my New Zealand winter wear was not going to cope with the cold Chicago weather. Even on the short walk I'd done that morning I had felt under-dressed. A new jacket and funky throw were soon purchased, along with some random other bits and pieces that I simply couldn't live without! As I walked around, I felt a growing admiration for the size and beauty of the city, which is so much grander than I was used to in Auckland.

Newly bundled up and cosy warm, I found my way back to the bistro I'd spotted earlier. Gorgeous box hedging enclosed this oasis of calm on the sidewalk, all crisp white linen tablecloths and sparkling silver and glassware, with the afternoon sun shining on the diners. Inside I was surprised to see how busy it was, a mixture of preppy guys and old ladies with fixed facial expressions and coiffed up-dos that looked like they'd been caught in a wind tunnel. I wanted to sit outside so that I could enjoy the autumn sunshine and as there was no queue for those tables I stuffed my shopping bags under the table out of sight, sat back and opened the menu.

Holy moly! I nearly fell off my chair when I saw the price of a glass of wine was $US 15. Reasoning that as it was my first day I could treat myself, and I was absolutely starving, I ordered a Cobb salad, fries and a glass of their finest chardonnay. Perfect. I could feel my nerves and anxiety slowly seeping away. As my meal arrived, I noticed the intertwined initials RL etched onto the side of the glass. Ralph Lauren. Aaaah, right, no wonder the prices looked steep, and no wonder it was the one place I had homed in on. Typical.

The food and wine were delicious, and I ordered another glass of wine but as the sun started to dip behind the skyline, the temperature likewise started to drop. With at least an hour of journey time ahead of me I headed back to the subway, vowing to visit again as soon as I could, and made my way back to the burbs and my miserable room. I felt really proud of myself for getting out rather than sitting around the motel feeling anxious, and happily had a much more positive Skype with Rob that evening.

Sunday morning brought a wake-up call again from the serenading car alarms and I cautiously opened the curtains to be greeted by another gorgeous blue-sky day.

I had planned to explore closer to home and practise my commute to the school, so I knew where I'd be going the next morning when classes started.

As it turned out, my commute would take me no more than 15 minutes walking, going past some extremely pretty weatherboard houses and through a small industrial estate with big wide roads and plenty of street lighting and no dark alleys – I could tell Dad later so he wouldn't worry unnecessarily. There was a supermarket en route and I popped in there on my way back to get some essentials. I have always loved going into supermarkets in foreign countries – there are always such interesting products and this one was no exception. I spent at least 10 minutes wandering up and down the fresh produce aisles and photographed a particularly unusual item called nopales, which looked distinctly like pieces off a giant cactus plant, and I had absolutely no idea how you would eat it. Channelling my student days I stocked up on bread, beans and some ready meals that could be heated easily in a microwave, and after about five minutes walking up and down the aisles I concluded that there were absolutely no screw top bottles of pinot noir, so I would have to invest in a bottle opener too.

The motel where I was staying had a diner attached and despite having just bought a small mountain of food, I decided to head in there and get something to take away and enjoy in my room. After a minor dilemma about how much of a tip to leave I was soon snuggled up in my warm room, wine poured, burger and fries plated, television on and Skype logged in ready for Rob. I didn't feel anywhere near as fraught as I had a couple of days earlier, but I was now starting to get a little nervous about the first day of the course, so Rob again found himself in the role of counsellor, reassuring me that I wasn't completely insane for what I was doing, and that everything would be fine!

Rob and I met 15 years ago through a mutual friend, Tom. Tom and I had shared a house together for three years when we were at university and had stayed in touch even though our lives had since taken us to live in different places – me to London and him to Cambridge. Tom had recently purchased a new house in Cambridge I had been promising to go and visit for months and kept delaying, I'm not sure why really. Life in London seemed to get in the way. Anyway, this weekend I did what I said I would do and drove up to see Tom and his girlfriend for the weekend. I had a vague memory of Tom mentioning he wanted to introduce me to his neighbour, but I hadn't really paid much attention to that. When I arrived, Tom said he'd arranged for us to go to a nearby pub to watch the rugby and his neighbour Rob would drive us. Tom's girlfriend then said she'd be interested to get my thoughts on this neighbour. She said he was really nice looking, seemed like a genuinely good guy but they weren't aware of any girlfriends. Must be gay I muttered and didn't think much more about it.

At the agreed time Rob arrived to drive us to the pub and after I'd managed to clamber my way onto the tiny back seat of a low sports car, I looked into the rear-view mirror and caught a pair of sharp ice-blue eyes looking back at me. Oooh, they're nice, I thought.

There followed a fun afternoon with lots of laughing and joking. After some hastily rearranged dinner plans Rob also came over for dinner at Tom's where the four of us had a fantastic evening.

Tom and his neighbours had organised a lunch for Sunday, the following day, which I went along to and Rob was also there. After lunch I drove back to London and later that evening Tom texted to ask whether he could give my number to Rob. "Of course you can!" I responded. Rob rang the next day and that Friday he travelled down to London where we had our first proper 'date'. The rest, as they say, is history.

Back to school

had been awake for ages, too excited to sleep. My nail varnish had been removed along with my jewellery, and I'd made sure my nails were cut short as per the course instructions. I was ready.

As I walked out through the motel reception doors into the early morning sunshine it was yet another truly gorgeous autumnal day. The air was cold and by the time I had crossed the first road my eyes were starting to sting with the cold. Despite that, I stopped to spend a few minutes watching a squirrel hopping along under a beautiful beech tree whose leaves were just starting to turn a deep golden colour with the change of the seasons. We don't have squirrels in New Zealand, so it reminded me of my childhood in the UK and I stood fixated for several minutes until I mentally shook myself and told myself to get to class!

I arrived at school with plenty of time to spare - as I always do. Even when I try to be late, I still end up being on time, or slightly early. It's one of the few things that really niggles between Rob and me. He will cut things fine and arrive just on time whereas I completely stress out if I think I'm going to be late. Thankfully this morning I wasn't the only one arriving early, one of the other attendees and his dog were already there, as was our instructor who was finishing setting up, with her dog.

"Hi, hi," I said and crouched down to talk to the dogs. I remembered my manners and shook hands with the instructor and we all exchanged polite greetings but I was so excited that when I started to talk my words kind of tumbled out of my mouth all over themselves, like I'd had too much caffeine, and I ended up mumbling and heading to take a seat to hide my embarrassment. The classroom was set up with a horseshoe of tables and each seat had a huge folder in front of it, waiting for its owner. I sat down and started leafing through the folder - clearly some serious work was about to start, and I could feel my nerves building again, what if I couldn't do this?

"On Saturday you will be providing pre and post event massage at an agility event being held here at the centre, and this week you will also be working on a two-legged Pit Bull."

I stared open-mouthed at our instructor as she announced the plan for the week. I looked around the room to see how everyone else had taken that little bombshell. And breathe.

There were five students in total, four women and one guy. During the initial introductions I had been excited to hear everyone's backgrounds. It turned out that most of us had come from the world of business, with only one person having any meaningful dog experience. Three were from the US, one from Canada and then me from the other side of the world. Everyone had seemed very intrigued that I had come all the way from New Zealand. We also had seven dogs in the room, a 12-year-old Border Collie Retriever mix who was deaf; a four-year-old Wheaten Terrier; two Shetland Sheepdogs; a young German Shepherd American Staffie mix, and a yellow Labrador, our instructor's dog. Immediately I loved the group, both humans and dogs.

My classmates had looked equally surprised by the instructor's announcement about what we would be doing in a week's time, but apart from that the day passed by extremely quickly and without incident. What was utterly fantastic but hard to believe is that we were 'hands-on' with some of the dogs that very first afternoon. To be in a classroom talking dogs with like-minded people and then getting to work on the dogs was my idea of heaven. The doubts and worries I had about what I was doing had completely disappeared by the end of the day.

Those first few days I blocked out my nerves about the prospect of working an agility event and on a two-legged Pit Bull and focused on learning the anatomy of the dog skeleton and major muscle groups. I was never much good at that kind of thing at school and trying to dig back to memories from school biology wasn't particularly helpful.

Being the only student from the UK my accent was a constant source of amusement, and I often repeated things, mainly because everyone enjoyed a little giggle at how I said things. Even the pronunciation of the word massage was entertaining – *mass*age versus mass*age*.

The building we were in was a warehouse which had been converted to a dog day-care centre. There was an area behind our classroom which housed several crates where the dogs would stay, and a large exercise area.

There was also a pool room for hydrotherapy treatments and at least half of the main area of the warehouse was a big open space which could be used for classes and agility events like the one we were going to be working at the following weekend. Our classroom was just off the reception area, which had loads of cool dog stuff for sale, and was sandwiched between that and the agility area.

Every day was hard work. I would get back to my room at the end of each day, completely exhausted. Classes started around 8am each morning, six days a week, finishing around 6pm, but frequently with the option to stay back and take part in further activity at the centre. Trying to keep up with everything that we were learning was challenging, but I was finding it so rewarding. I had started a blog before I left New Zealand and I made sure I updated that regularly – I wanted to be able to look back on this experience and remember how I felt at the time, what we covered, and to have a record of everything.

Back in New Zealand, Rob and I would Skype as often as we could, and I managed to watch online as he competed in the Coastal Classic Yacht race, and also was able to get updates on Asha and her friends at her boarding facility, running free and having fun.

Blog extract from Tuesday, 14 October 2014

Awesome!
I can't believe that we got 'hands on' with the dogs on Day One. It was Awesome. We've spent a lot of time over the last two days talking about the principles of massage i.e. feeling with fingers rather than brains which is lot harder than you think 'cause your brain automatically tries to analyse and name what it is you are feeling; and most importantly about understanding the dogs. That's hard. But you have to have respect and empathy when you are working with dogs and to do that you need to be able to understand them. There's a lady called Suzanne Clothier who sounds amazing, YouTube her if you get a chance.
We did some energy work yesterday which ordinarily I would have laughed at but I could actually feel the energy from the dog – a difference between hot and cold in certain places – which was again... awesome. [Note to self to find another descriptor ;)]
Apparently on Saturday we will be doing 1:1 sports massages on some agility dogs... Holy S*&t!!!!!
Am now sipping some pinot noir in my hotel room and reflecting on Day Two where it was more hands-on work, learning about the nervous and integumentary systems, low stress handling and behaviour observation.
Low stress handling is huge. Not only for dogs that have an injury but for shelter dogs, those who are touch

resistant for whatever reason, and those that are highly excitable. It's vitally important to gain their trust before any kind of hands-on happens. One thing is to imagine how you feel when you're in a totally new place and don't know anyone (this hit home for me especially after my turbulent weekend!), and then try and imagine how a dog feels when it's in a shelter or is being re-homed.

Over the course of the week I had purposely put the thought of the impending agility event out of my mind. One step at a time I told myself, however as the week progressed, we started to learn more and gradually my confidence was increasing. All too quickly the end of that first week arrived and the agility event was no longer a distant challenge – it was happening the very next day.

I felt a bit anxious waking up that day and as I headed to the Windy City Agility Club.

I could feel the excitement and energy level as soon as I walked into the club. The area outside our classroom had been transformed into an agility course, all bright colours and a dizzying array of equipment with one side reserved as the waiting area for the dogs. Some were in their crates, others sitting with their owners. Some were barking excitedly, some sitting calmly. The noises and anticipation were an assault on my senses, and I felt super-nervous. We had been working on dogs all week but there were a lot of people and dogs here and this felt very different.

We were each paired with an instructor and given a room to work in for the next few hours. My first client was a four-year-old Border Collie. I took a couple of deep calming breaths as he walked in with his owner. I don't know who was more on edge, me or him. Be patient, I told myself, let him relax and get used to my touch. I had a brief chat with the owner who told me his dog was a little shy and had never had a massage before. I mentally crossed my inexperienced fingers and prayed that I didn't put him off for life. "Breathe," I told myself, as I worked extremely gently and calmly so that by the end of his short time with me, he was sitting in my lap while I released tension in his back legs. My relief was immense. After a few more clients we had a group debrief with our instructors and then I headed back to my motel, floating on cloud nine but utterly shattered!

As there was no school the next day, I allowed myself a sleep in before tackling the laundromat. It had been a very, very long time since I had visited a laundromat and this one made any previous experiences pale in comparison. This place had over 100 machines, and it was full of families doing their weekly washing. I lugged my two carrier bags of washing up and down the aisles until I found a machine that looked vacant and started loading my washing.

"Move on honey, that one's mine," came a voice from behind me. I looked round to see a middle-aged woman with two kids in tow and so much washing that she would obviously be there all afternoon. The competition for machines was fierce.

I apologised profusely and moved on to find another machine. It's amazing how much washing you can generate in a week when your clothes are either covered in dog slobber, hair and unfortunately in my case a patch of wee on one knee where I'd inadvertently knelt in a puddle. Looking around, everyone had come equipped. They had their own laundry baskets, clothes rails and bags. I was not as well prepared and put my clean but wet laundry back into the plastic bags and started the search for an available dryer. Waiting for my clothes had been a fascinating exercise in people-watching but I was for once pleased to get back to my motel room and some peace and quiet.

Each day I was reminded of what an absolute treat it was to be among like-minded people who loved nothing more that talking dog all day.

In my previous job my favourite work colleague had coined the phrase 'dog Tourette's' for me. We had travelled to Christchurch for business one time and driving around the park I had suddenly shouted out "DOG!" at some people exercising their dog in the park so that he'd look over and see them. A couple of seconds later I had done it again. "You seriously have dog Tourette's," Jake said. We both thought that was hilarious, but it was spot on. I have never been one of those people who would coo or fawn over a baby in a pushchair walking down the street – I never notice them. Dogs on the other hand are a different matter. I notice them all, small ones, large ones, puppies, geriatrics, you name it, I'll find the dogs.

When we got our dog Asha, people would often comment as they walked by, normally something like "cute pup" or "ohhh isn't she gorgeous" and I would smile indulgently and agree with them. Now that is me, I can't walk past a dog without saying something or asking if it's ok to have a pat if I have time to stop. I love them all!

Thankfully as classmates we progressed quickly from the first couple of days when we were a little bit on edge and shy to being totally comfortable with each other. I really enjoyed the group, we laughed a lot, and everyone was very kind to each other. There was one time when we all got a bit flustered... Our instructor, being a qualified human massage therapist as well as a canine one, was obviously completely comfortable massaging humans. Us not so much. The first time she had told us to pair up (fully clothed of course) and practise compression and finding knots on each other's shoulders we immediately reverted to our initial shyness.

She told us to pair up so three of us were sitting on chairs and the others were standing behind. I was paired with Scott (who was from Dallas and the lone guy on the course) so was standing behind him, hands on his shoulders. Scott and I had become friends very early on in the course however I still felt like I was back at junior school and that kind of nervous giggling light-headedness that starts to build up when you're self-conscious. Being English as well, we're not big on touch so putting my hands on a relative stranger felt very strange. I took a deep breath and followed the directions, feeling gently for knots and working around Scott's shoulders and along his back. I could feel my face going red and started getting really hot, my posture just didn't seem right, and I felt flustered. I could feel myself trying to suppress that nervous giggle and looking right I could see my neighbour was struggling and doing the same thing.

"Don't forget to breathe," announced our instructor and with a collective sigh we all breathed out and started to laugh. I hadn't realised I was holding my breath and immediately started to feel calmer and got my focus back.

On another occasion we worked on one of the employees at the centre who was having knee issues. The poor girl had to roll up her trousers and submit herself to five sets of inexperienced hands learning how to do lymphatic drainage work. She was lovely, absolutely nothing wrong with her at all, but truly, touching humans isn't my bag, give me a dog any time!

To break up the classroom work of theory and practical massage we also had some class outings to visit local shelters. The shelter work was really special for me and whilst we only saw a very small number of the dogs that were staying at them – we were basically just trust building, observing gait and where possible providing some massage – it was clear to see that the dogs enjoyed the interaction and gained some relief from our work whilst living under what must be stressful conditions for them.

Fifty

O k, ok, everyone stand up and take three deep breaths," said our instructor over the din in the room.

It was just after lunch and the dogs in the class were having a wonderful time as we were all chatting loudly and laughing. The Wheaten Terrier was beside himself with excitement, bouncing up into the air on all four feet whilst two others were wrestling on the carpet at the front of the class. I was missing my dog Asha and wondered what she would be doing if she were in the room right now. Probably joining in the wrestling with the two at the front. The Shetland Sheepdogs were sitting politely together, and the elderly gentleman was refusing to eat his fish oil tablet. Just normal lunchtime shenanigans and I was loving it

We all stood up as directed and as we started to take our deep breaths, I could feel the energy in the room starting to calm down. Incredibly by the end of the third breath we were all feeling calmer and the dogs had stopped bounding around.

The dogs were put away into their crates and the door opened to allow the two-legged Pit Bull, Fifty, to come in – a moment I had been waiting patiently for, for days.

As he came into the room, I could feel my eyes welling up (I am so hopeless!), how is this even possible I wondered.

I continued to watch him walking around as we heard the story of how he had been shot when he was only two years old. My eyes were not deceiving me, this was who we had been promised earlier in the week.

This was Fifty.

Around 20kg of gorgeous lean light brown Pit Bull was hopping steadily and confidently around our classroom, checking for any doggy delicacies that might be lurking under the desks or in the corners of the room.

From the moment I heard about this legendary Pit Bull, I had been dying to meet him. I hadn't really known what to expect. We hadn't asked which two legs he had, so when he came in it was the first time we'd seen his ability. The result of his early trauma was that he was missing both legs on the right side of his body. He had a bit of a stump for his right hind leg, but his right front was completely missing. On hearing the story of how this happened I don't think there was a dry eye in the classroom.

Before I arrived in Chicago, I had been apprehensive about meeting a real-life Pit Bull. They get such bad press and I guess I had to some degree believed the hype. Since arriving in Chicago and starting the course my opinion had completely changed – we were taught to meet the dog, not the breed. This made such sense to me and during the time on the course I had been lucky enough to watch a practice session for a couple of dancing dogs – a dancing duo of Pit Bull and Toy Poodle where the Toy Poodle balanced on the other's back, a unique sight to behold!

We all sat in a semi-circle on the floor and watched Fifty's progress around the room. He hopped steadily on his remaining two legs, using his tail as a rudder. It was truly incredible to see how this dog was managing to navigate around. He was surprisingly stable and when he finally finished his exploring he came over to the group. Treats in hand we all happily dispensed them to Fifty. I simply couldn't take my eyes off him as he sat in front of me, soulful eyes gazing into my face with a big wide grin while he gently took treats from my fingers with his soft muzzle.

Once the treats had been exhausted, he slumped down on the floor in front of us ready for his massage. Let's be clear here, this dog was a massage pro – since his current owner had adopted him several years before, he had received regular massage, physiotherapy, hydrotherapy and laser so he knew what was good for him. He further amazed me by willingly allowing himself to be poked and prodded by our inexperienced hands. Feeling his tail, which he used to balance himself, you could feel the tightness in the muscles – quite unlike any tail I had felt before.

With over 250,000 followers on Facebook, Fifty was an ambassador for Pit Bulls and a bit of a celebrity in the Chicago canine rehabilitation world. It was unlikely that he would have lived for so long without the myriad of treatments that he received

With Fifty lying on the floor in front of me waiting for more hands-on work I was seriously happy.

Thanks Chicago

Nearly four weeks later and my course was coming to an end. I was sad to be leaving the school and saying goodbye to my new friends. The course had been absolutely incredible, but I was now ready to get back home and get my newly educated fingers to work on our dog Asha. Whilst we had managed to Skype lots, and Rob had regularly sent me pictures of our ginger stick monster – one of Asha's many nicknames, this particular one chosen for her colouring and the enormous delight she found in anything related to sticks – I was hugely missing them both.

To keep me company for my last few days in Chicago, Debbie was flying over from the UK. Debbie and I have been best friends since our very first week at university when we bonded on a coach trip over discussions about what to wear to the first-year ball. Even though for the last few years we'd lived on opposite sides of the world, whenever we see each other it's as if we have never been apart and we just pick up where we left off. When I'd told Debbie I was going to Chicago I'd half-jokingly suggested she come and see me. I hadn't wanted to get my hopes up in case it didn't happen, but as soon as she emailed to let me know her flights were booked, I let myself get into full on excitement mode.

One of my classmates gave me a lift to the airport to pick her up and then I had the joy of showing off my miserable motel room, which seemed considerably brighter with Debs in it. Within five minutes we had our PJs on and were sitting on the bed with a bag of crisps and a bottle of wine between us, catching up on all our news. Debs is an amazingly thoughtful friend and she had brought me a bag of British goodies (she did a similar thing when Rob and I had left for New Zealand many years ago). Like a 'tuck box' that kids go off to boarding school or camp with, this box was crammed full of all the best things from home and with the company of my much-loved friend both my soul and stomach were feeling well-nourished. After hours of talking, a shared dinner and several silly selfies we finally dozed off and it seemed that in no time the alarm was going off and it was my final day of the course.

Over the last few weeks I had been gradually adding more and more layers of clothing to my outfits to keep out the cold on my early morning walk to school. I was about to suggest to Debs that she 'layer up' when she unveiled what could only be described as a duvet masquerading as a coat – I had serious coat envy. Yet again, it was cold and bright as we walked to class and within minutes we had tears streaming down our faces from the biting wind.

"Just come on in and sit at the back of the class," I said to Debs once we arrived.

"Will there be dogs in there?" she asked me.

"Yes… just a couple," I lied, knowing where the conversation was going.

"How many is that?"

"Probably about six," I smiled sheepishly.

"Forget it," she said with a laugh. "I'll wait outside in reception."

Debs is not a dog person which is not helped by the fact that she is mildly allergic to their hair, so I found her a chair in the reception area with the promise that I'd be finished in a couple of hours and she settled in to check her emails.

Today we were only going to have a few last-minute things to cover off in class. It felt very strange to be saying goodbye to everyone I had become so close to over the last few weeks, and I was surprised how sad I felt. Once I was back in New Zealand, I would be so far away from everyone and I would miss this supportive group as I took my next steps on this journey. We all promised to stay in touch and to help each other with the work assignments that needed to be completed and assessed before we could gain our certification. My class-mate Scott, from Dallas, was going to be my 'study buddy' and we arranged to Skype when I got home so we could support each other through all that work.

At the end of the class we took a group photo, goodbyes were said, and we were off, back out in the cold and heading to the miserable motel for the very last time. We'd booked an Airbnb for the next week and I couldn't wait to get to it.

Despite only having arrived the night before, Debbie's suitcase had managed to spill its entire contents all over the floor of my room and we both had to sit on it to get it to close. I had also invested in an additional suitcase for all my extra purchases (including three new collars and a dog bed for Asha, not to mention all the hair products I had loaded up on).

The pictures we'd seen of our Airbnb online did not disappoint. A gorgeous little terrace in downtown Chicago, which had once been a shop, in a super-cute neighbourhood. We dumped our bags and belongings in the middle of the floor and immediately headed out to explore Chicago.

First stop on our whistle-stop itinerary was Soho House, part of the exclusive Soho House brand of upmarket hotels, for a pedicure and lunch which was pure decadence. I'd spent the last three and a half weeks living in trainers, jeans and jumpers with little or no makeup on, covered in dog hair, and coming home to a dreary room – Soho House was a dream in comparison.

We washed down our artisan pizzas with some cocktails, before wandering towards the river to see the city by boat. Being a Wednesday, the boat was relatively empty, so we sat on the top deck at the back and warmed our hands on cups of steaming tea. It was late afternoon and the sun was beginning to set behind the skyscrapers and the air was getting decidedly chilly. Despite Debbie's duvet coat and my layering of clothes we were soon both cold, even huddled under a blanket that the boat's captain had loaned us. We were so cold that we didn't move for the whole entire trip, but the view was breathtaking, the sky was clear and learning about the architecture and history of the city was amazing. Chicago had never been somewhere I'd thought of visiting but it is such a gorgeous city. Once the tour finished, we prised ourselves off our seats and quickly went in search of warmth and more liquid sustenance.

Debs is a great person to travel with, she researches and hunts out the best places to go so that over the next few days we enjoyed shopping, sightseeing, eating, drinking and generally catching up. Years earlier she had visited me in New York where I had been living. There was a burger bar opposite my apartment building but in the months I'd been living there I hadn't ventured in; a) because it looked ever so slightly seedy and I was in my 'Sex in the City' era, all Tiffany and heels; and b) I was a bit nervous about going in there on my own.

"Come on. We're going over to get a burger," Debs had insisted. It turned out to be fantastic. We sat at the bar with our bottles of beer and watched the burgers cooking on the grill behind. It remains one of the best burgers I have ever eaten.

This trip was no different.

In the few days we had in Chicago, we ate doughnuts at 1am, shopped until we dropped in Walgreens, ate pancakes, maple syrup and bacon in a classic diner, took selfies in front of Chicago's famous Bean, and generally walked miles and miles exploring the fabulous city.

But, as the saying goes, all good things must come to an end. We each sat on our suitcases to get them to close, headed to the airport and Debs went one way and I another.

Duke

I sat in the car outside the address of my very first 'solo' client and practised my relaxed breathing, desperately trying to calm myself.

Duke, a gorgeous yellow Labrador had been referred to me by a friend, and having met him once I knew that he was a lovable old gentleman who thoroughly enjoyed a good pat.

"He will totally love it," my friend had said after she had ok'd it with Mary (his owner) that I could use him as one of my five case studies.

"He's getting on a bit now and is looking a little stiff when he walks, he is definitely slowing down," his owner had informed me when I'd called to arrange the appointment.

Arriving early, I sat outside their house, my little notebook crammed full of notes from Chicago in my lap, flicking through the pages to the highlighted sections for tips I had scribbled down. I had the radio on and Taylor

Swift's "Shake it Off" was playing – how apt I mused as I tried to shake off my nerves and ensure that I was purely focused on Duke.

Not that there is anything to be nervous about, I self-talked. It's just Duke, you've met him, he'll be great. As I had another four dogs to work on for my case studies, I was pleased that Duke would be my first one as I hadn't met any of the others. Ease myself in gently I thought (yeah right!)

I finally mustered the courage to go in and Duke duly greeted me at the door, smiling from ear to ear. Mary his owner led me through to the lounge where I set up my mat. I ran through the standard intake questionnaire we had been given in Chicago and discovered that Duke had started life as an assistance dog for the blind, but sadly he had become rather stressed and had been re-homed to Mary and her family. At 10 years old he had now been with them for about five years. In hindsight my alarm bells should have gone off then, but I wasn't listening properly, I still had the 'he will love it, such a smoochy boy' loop playing in my head.

Mary checked that I was ok and then went back to the kitchen table where she was finishing off a marketing presentation. I focused my attention on Duke who was now sitting in front of me, gazing into my face. I commenced the massage as I had been taught to do, however after only about five minutes Duke was becoming restless. He had started panting and kept shifting from one hip to another. I tried to get him to lie down in front of me, but he wasn't having any of it.

"Everything all right over there?" inquired Mary.

"Yep, all good thanks," I responded as I tried to calm my breathing and work out how I could relax Duke.

After a few more minutes I let him get up, so he could have a drink of water.

He came back over to me afterwards and sat in front of me again, looking up at me.

"You're ok Duke," I crooned at him, but the moment I started to touch him again he started panting and this time started licking his lips as he looked at me – sure signs of discomfort.

"Is it ok if I give him some treats?" I asked Mary. "He's looking a little stressed."

"Sure, he'll love some treats," said Mary as she came over and sat on the sofa in a bid to help him calm down.

So, I tried treats. But again, the stress signals were up. I started getting flustered. What was I doing wrong? I could feel myself getting a bit hot and bothered.

I continued to try and calm him however it was clear to both Mary and I that the type of touch that he was receiving from me was not something he was comfortable with.

"I can't believe it, I thought he'd just love it," said Mary fondly. "What a weirdo."

We wrapped up the session and I arranged to come back in a week for his next session.

To be honest I felt pretty gutted. It was my first session on my own and it had not gone well. Oh, dear I thought (not for the first time) what have I done?

I spent a fair bit of time reflecting on the session and it wasn't until 3am a few nights later that I woke up with it dawning on me that I simply hadn't listened to Duke. Rookie error, I thought to myself. All my time in human resources had taught me to be observant of people and hear what they were saying, really hear them not just listen, and I had just done the exact opposite. Mary had told me he had a tendency to be stressed and yet I had ignored that and gone at the pace I had wanted, not taking enough notice of what Duke was saying.

I approached my second session with Duke very differently. I sat in the car outside again and looked through my notes, but when I went inside, I really tried to listen to Duke. I went a lot more slowly with him, focusing on keeping very calm and measuring my breathing so it was deliberate and methodical, allowing Duke to gradually become accustomed to me and my touch. This worked so much better and over the following couple of appointments Duke's acceptance of touch from me improved enormously. In each session he relaxed a little more and panted less and less. I was learning to be patient and go at the dog's pace, something that would become a bit of a mantra in the following months and years. Duke had taught me a very valuable lesson and I will always be grateful to him for that.

Home sweet home

T o obtain my certification from Chicago I needed to complete a number of observation hours and case studies, so I had been busy trying to build my network of dog people. Starting from scratch on a new career is pretty daunting and during my research I had found just three other people in the whole of New Zealand who were practising dog massage. I needed to put myself out there and try and make as many connections as possible.

Using my newly established network (more on that later!) I arranged to spend a few mornings at a dog day-care centre to satisfy the requirement for my observation hours. What an eye-opener that was. Dogs of all different sizes, breeds and ages having an absolute ball! It gave me a newfound respect for anyone working at a doggy day-care, it was utterly exhausting. On your feet for hours, eyes in the back of your head, picking up poo and mopping up wee. I admit I loved it and being able to watch the dogs interacting – watching how they 'talked' to each other – was amazing. I'd never spent that much time simply watching. The occasional scuffle had to be diffused and a couple of 'zoomies' intercepted before the energy in the room got the chance to spiral out of control (best described as the pure joy on the part of the 'zoomer' who tucks in their tail and literally zooms around the area at a rate of knots enticing the others to chase after them). I noted a couple of dogs stressing slightly so spent a little time with them practising some calming techniques. The team were extremely knowledgeable about the behaviour of the dogs and pointed out things to me that the untrained eye might miss – a swish of a tail, a shift in posture, a lick of the lips or a tilt of the ears.

Armed with this newfound knowledge I headed off to my local dog park one day. It's not somewhere Rob and I tend to go with Asha but on this occasion, I wanted to watch my own dog and see how obvious or otherwise her signals were. At one point she found a youngish Spaniel to play with. I was chatting to the owner whilst keeping one eye on Asha. I could see (and hear) that she was getting more and more excited, so I tried to intercept and command some 'time out'. No chance, Asha was well and truly in the zone. She and the other dog were racing round but I noticed a distinct change in the manner of play when the other dog tried to hide under a bush. I took the opportunity to grab Asha.

"They're ok," said the other guy. "They're just having fun."

"Nah, I'm not so sure they are now," I said. "My dog is being a bit of a monkey, trying to bully yours, and yours is trying to get away!"

He looked surprised by this but accepted it and we headed our separate ways.

It was a happy day when I finally received my certificate from Chicago, having completed all the relevant case studies, observation hours and tests. Next all I had to do was pass the exams to get my National Board Certification in Animal Acupressure and Massage (NBCAAM). I mean, I didn't HAVE to sit any more exams, but I really did want to be taken seriously so wanted the extra certification. None of the three other people in New Zealand doing canine massage had this particular qualification so I figured it would be a unique selling point for me. Scott, my friend from the course in Chicago, and I spent many hours Skyping between Dallas and Auckland, testing each other in preparation for the exams. We set ourselves weekly tasks for subjects to cover and then quizzed each other. We had some past exam questions and topics to practise with – it was hard, but it was great to support each other. We'd both gained our certificates from the school in Chicago but the stuff we needed to know for the NBCAAM was a lot more in-depth. After a solid few months of studying we both passed and could now call ourselves Nationally Certified.

In between studying I had been continuing to spread the word about canine massage with anyone and everyone I met.

I caught up with Alex, the practice owner of my own vet clinic who is a cool guy and obviously very busy. I'd be lying if I didn't admit that I was ever so slightly intimidated to be meeting up with a vet, especially because I really wanted him to endorse what I did and ideally, I wanted to work out of his clinic.

I met him as arranged, at the clinic.

"Will this take long?"

Great start. "No, it won't take long but I do really want to talk with you."

"Ok. Let's go out and get a coffee."

We walked out of the clinic and headed to a coffee shop up the road. As soon as we were outside, he said, "Tell me."

I took a deep breath and explained about my background, the qualification I now had and the benefits of massage for dogs. By the time we got to the coffee shop he had relaxed, and we were having a good discussion.

Cautiously I broached the subject of a room and asked him for his thoughts.

"Well I have to admit to being a bit sceptical," he said. "We had a healer working with us for a little while but all they seemed to do was get into the cages with the dogs and lay down with them." He smiled. "They only lasted a few weeks."

I didn't want to disrespect anyone, but I explained to him that my approach was quite pragmatic!

We finished our coffees and by the time we parted ways I really felt like he was on board. He asked me to come up with some words to go in the next clinic newsletter. I was beyond chuffed.

I carried on building and expanding my network of connections in the canine industry. I was pleasantly surprised how supportive most people seemed to be. After the initial uncertainty, people understood the benefits and I became an expert with the 'elevator pitch' we'd drafted in Chicago. We'd all laughed and joked our way through the session where we had come up with our three-minute elevator pitches but that practice really did come in handy. Basically what this meant was if you were in a lift or elevator with someone and you wanted to explain (and sell) what you did to that person in a very small amount of time, how on earth would you say what you did. I'd had a fair bit of practice at being concise in my previous career, I remember one business manager demanding I talk to him about the merits of whatever human resources thing I was trying to discuss, whilst I accompanied him to the toilet. Not into it obviously, but I had only two minutes from leaving his desk, walking around the trading floor, down the corridor and to the door of the toilet. Translate that to canine massage and keeping someone's attention in a busy bar or gaining their interest in the first couple of minutes of meeting. I had to be succinct.

It was incredibly daunting to be the only one doing this in Auckland, but I felt like I'd made it when I was invited to join a newly set up group for female veterinary professionals and those working closely with the vets such as animal physiotherapists. The first meeting I attended I was pretty tense and had to keep reminding myself that whilst I considered myself merely a massage therapist in amongst these incredible vet professionals, in all likelihood I did in fact know more than they did about massage. Keeping that thought with me to get through the initial introductory part of the meeting, I ended up making some really great contacts with people who would eventually become good friends.

I guess it's not the first time I've taken a rather large plunge into the unknown. Eleven years ago, Rob and I moved all our worldly belongings across the globe from the UK to New Zealand, to start afresh. We'd never been to New Zealand before but figured, "What the heck, what have we got to lose? If we don't like it, we can just come home." Fighting talk!

Rob and I both shared a desire to live in another country for a while. I'd already spent time living briefly in New York and Milan and was interested in a change again. Originally, we thought about moving to Australia. My brother and his girlfriend were already talking about moving to Perth and we were close to joining them... until we went on our honeymoon to the Cook Islands and met a couple from New Zealand.

Over dinner with our new friends Nikki and Dennis, we talked about our dreams and plans to move to Australia.

"Why would you want to go there?" asked Nikki and Dennis together.

"Well, my brother is going to live there, the weather is amazing, and we really enjoyed it when we visited a couple of years ago," I responded.

"What about New Zealand, have you thought about going there?"

"No, we don't really know much about it, we didn't get across there when we did our two months around Australia, so we've never been."

"You should consider it. It's like England 20 years ago, and we don't have the nasties that Australia has."

"Nasties?"

"Yeah, we don't have any nasty snakes and spiders, in fact we don't have any snakes at all."

Having a phobia about snakes my ears immediately pricked up and I looked over at Rob. "We should totally look into it," I said emphatically to him.

Two years later almost to the day I was standing in our friend's kitchen in Surrey in a kind of terror trance, thinking about the enormity of what we were about to do the following day. Our flight was leaving early afternoon, so we were packed and ready to go. It was honestly so incredibly scary that I felt like my mind had stopped working and everything was on autopilot. The word the Swedish have for it is 'Resfeber' – literally translated as travel fever: "The restless race of the traveller's heart before the journey begins," (so an internet translation explains). That evening and most of the following day are a blur but I distinctly remember ringing my brother and his wife in Perth, from London's Heathrow airport, and panic breathing down the phone at them.

"You've done the hardest part," said Susie. "Now you can just enjoy it!"

Those few simple words had a hugely calming effect on me, and I relaxed.

Twenty-four hours later we arrived in our new home. We had two cases each and knew two people.

That first day Rob and I were keen to explore our new home town of Auckland. We walked for miles, enjoying the beautiful spring weather, before settling in to eat fish and chips in a pretty waterfront bistro, basking in the glorious sunshine. Sadly, we weren't prepared for the fierceness of the New Zealand sun and returned to our hotel with rather red sunburnt faces. Happily, that had calmed down by day three, the day of the seafood festival. Before we had left the UK, a New Zealand friend had given us the contact details of his sister who lived in Auckland. We had an email exchange and arranged to meet at a seafood festival a couple of days after we arrived.

We'd organised to meet our friend's sister and her husband in a bar before going to the festival and upon meeting we immediately clicked. She then introduced us into a group of their friends, and we have all remained close ever since. The next day Nikki and Dennis travelled to Auckland to spend the day with us and by the end of our first weekend Rob and I knew we would be ok.

PART 2

Setting Up

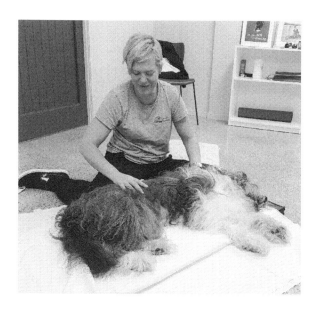

Me with Reeve, an English Bearded Collie, in one of my clinics.

Where to start?

I had never been driven to own or run my own business and had always quite enjoyed the fact that someone else had all the responsibility. I would turn up for work where the computer, phone etc would be provided for me (along with the all-important technical support), business cards would arrive and all the other jazz that goes with being a good employee.

Having to think of all this myself was quite intimidating. It was also really important to me to set the right tone, everything needed to be properly branded. Starting with the name.

When I was in Chicago I had played with several names, mulling them over to see what worked best and resonated the most with me. I really couldn't decide however and when I asked people, over dinner, coffee or just randomly, I got mixed responses. So, I decided to employ some of my human resources skills and planned a 'name-storming' evening with the brightest and most creative minds I could find – i.e. my closest girlfriends.

Running a brainstorming session was something I'd done a few times but if felt quite different to be doing it for myself, and not on someone else's behalf. I managed to acquire a flip chart pad, a whole load of brightly coloured marker pens and Post-it notes. I also invested in those good old focus tools of wine and cheese.

I felt a bit nervous as I looked round my living room at my friends – I had a lot riding on this and I really wanted to make it a worthwhile session, both for them and me. Rob was standing by as the token male and before I knew it, I was giving my spiel at the front of the group, explaining what my vision and purpose was. We went through a series of exercises with me sticking up Post-it notes on the walls and flip charts around the room. Everyone was engaged and focused with loads and loads of ideas, from the clearly inappropriate (Happy Doggy Endings), to the more possible (Healing Hounds), to my favourite (Auckland Canine Massage). I had pondered this particular name for a while but ultimately it says what it is and for me that was very important when I was setting out in such a new business area.

Next on the agenda was a logo. I had an idea that I wanted to try and incorporate something of Asha in the logo if possible and got in touch with a friend to develop it. Now I do not consider myself a creative person at all, I'm simply not that way inclined. My brother and mother are the creatives in my family so when Ani, my very patient designer, asked me if I had any ideas I felt completely unhelpful trying to describe what it was I was after. Despite my inarticulation, she listened to what I wanted the brand to stand for and came back with eight potential sketches that were all good.

Rob got home one day from work to find giant logos stuck on the kitchen cupboards.

"What do you reckon babe?" I asked.

"They're all good, I like them all." Great to hear but not really what I was looking for.

"Yes, but if you had to choose, which one would it be?"

He grabbed a beer from the fridge and propped himself up against the sink to contemplate the group of designs.

"Third one down."

"Oh really? I like the second one down." Marvellous.

These designs accompanied me everywhere I went for a good two weeks. Friends must have thought I was mad when mid-coffee or supper I would whip out the designs and ask them "Which one?" Finally, we landed on the design and the colours, and I was so happy.

Next came the business cards, flyers and posters.

For a second time I went to see Alex, the practice manager of my local vet, this time with business cards. He gave me his seal of approval and I was so relieved – it was a big deal to get his approval on the professionalism of my branding and it gave me a huge confidence boost.

I sent a few samples of my cards and flyers to my Mum and Dad in the UK and to my brother in Australia, so they could all share in my joy!

Next came a uniform. I'd been impressed in Chicago with the smart polo shirts and t-shirts we'd been given, and I decided that although I didn't want to be too formal, I did need a uniform of some sort. I love clothes. I spend a lot of time devouring the pages of gorgeous outfits in my favourite weekly UK magazine. My old business wardrobe had already been vacuum packed away in the loft as there wasn't a single thing there that would be suitable for my new career. I trotted along to my local shopping mall to look at uniform options. I kind of knew what I wanted, a grey or black t-shirt, some grey or black pants and a pair of slip-on trainers. Clothes that were easy to wear and wash and shoes that I could easily take on and off for visiting dogs at home, with no laces for dogs to chew on. I struck gold in one of the shops and got the whole lot, including a jacket and sweatshirt I could brand as well.

Excited as I was with my new choice of clothing it was a tough day when I finally took a load of my old business wardrobe to the charity shop. I had to do it, part of starting something new is saying goodbye to the old, right? I carefully chose pieces that I thought someone else would find useful and handed my previously beloved garments over for their next journey. Incredibly I even managed to part with a couple of pairs of shoes that I knew I would not need again.

Once the basics of the name, business cards, flyers and posters and uniform could be ticked off the list I needed to turn my thoughts to the more technical side of creating a business.

Having said I don't have a creative bone in my body, I actually enjoyed organising and arranging all the design aspects of my new business. I enjoyed it SO much more than setting up the business processes. Thank goodness for Rob. Rob is a computer programmer, so processes and analytics come very naturally to him. He is at pains to remind me that he is not my tech support guy, in fact his skill set is very different, and he doesn't really understand computers the way a tech support person would, however it still makes more sense to him than it does to me. I have no patience. It's something that's well understood within my family. Whenever my mother needs some help with Skype, or her emails, or whatever it is to do with her computer, it has to be Rob who talks to her. I simply can't do it; we both end up cross and frustrated and I additionally end up racked with guilt for being so impatient with my mum.

A typical conversation with Rob will be, "Hey Rob, can you come and help me, this stupid computer won't work properly," as he just walks through the door. Rob being the incredibly kind and tolerant man that he is will wander through to the office – with a wagging, toy carrying ginger stick monster in tow – head cocked to one side, and say, "What's happened babe? Move over and let me have a look." I hands-down consider myself the luckiest girl alive.

When I started to set up some processes for tracking clients, money and appointments, Rob was there to help me. But oh my goodness don't get me started on the domain name. The bunch of code that came up in front of me when I tried to sort this out left me reeling with confusion and even took Rob a good few hours to navigate. Patience and persistence won in the end, and we worked it out using the help we found from other users on the internet.

I think one of my proudest moments was when my car got branded. I hadn't however really thought through the implications for my driving style.

I distinctly remember a previous manager I worked with dealing with a complaint from a member of the public about one of our employees' driving. The email went something like "… and remember if you are going to behave like a petrol head you have a number written along the side of your car which basically says "Call my boss"… " The last thing I wanted was for my reputation to be trashed based on my driving. But driving a branded car was like driving in a goldfish bowl – every time we drove past my local café, I thought everyone was staring at me.

I stopped at lights in town once and some guys were crossing the road in front of me and when they caught sight of the name and logo on my car, they started nudging each other and laughing whilst pointing at me. I smiled to myself thinking, "Sure you go ahead, laugh all you like... and then go and tell everyone you know about this thing you saw, spread the word for me". The power of word of mouth!

Blog excerpt from Thursday, 12 March 2015

Stats and Stories...

2038   Blog page views
13   Days since Auckland Canine
              Massage has been officially
              open for business
348   Number of days since I first
              discovered canine massage was
              a thing
15   Days since website and
              Facebook page went live
128   Facebook likes
171   Days since my first blog post
6   Average age of my current
              four-legged client base
Hundreds The hours of canine massage I
              have performed

I've been asked a few times over the last week how and why I got into this field and over dinner this week a friend asked me whether I had exhibited any behaviours when I was younger that suggested I might eventually find myself massaging dogs for a living.
When I asked my mum, she confirmed that as a child I always loved dogs. Apparently, aged six, I used to say that our English Cocker Spaniel (Misty) was MY dog, and I would get extremely upset when on returning from school and taking her for a walk as soon as I let her off the lead in the field she would run home to my mother! Mum was at home; I was at school – makes sense now right.
I was never afraid of dogs despite being bitten by a very cute West Highland

White Terrier when I was about five – it was totally my fault! I'd been told repeatedly not to touch strange dogs and especially not to put my hand through fences and gates to touch them, but I did – the little hand went through the gate and the dog bit me. He broke the skin but there was no lasting damage! Mum also remembered a time when I was allowed to walk their friends' Springer Spaniel on the lead and was practically airborne with him pulling me down the lane.

The joys of Social Media

Y ou need Facebook, Twitter, Instagram and Snapchat everyone said. For a start, what even is Snapchat and what on earth would I, a canine massage therapist, have to Tweet about?

It made me feel anxious and grumpy just thinking about all these different platforms; it seemed overwhelming. Of course, I wanted to be accessible to as many people as possible but if I did all this, I seriously wouldn't have time for anything else. I decided to start with something that was vaguely familiar, or so I thought... Facebook. What a drama. You'd think it would be easy and straightforward but no. First of all, I needed a different app. Then I needed to decide how to categorise my business. Then you had to upload profile and background pictures and of course my logo wouldn't fit and had to be tweaked slightly. Then came the wording.

My sister-in-law had recently started her own business in the UK, so I jumped onto her business page to see what I could learn. She has a background in public relations and marketing so hers looked really good. I looked back at my pitiful attempt and re-wrote everything and chose different photos. Midway through all this I got a like. Panic! What the...? How had that happened? NO! I'm not ready, I'm not ready yet! I checked to see who had liked it. My brother, phew, breathe, relax, that was ok. I calmed down and focused on getting the page finished.

But then what would my first post be? Would it be "Welcome followers"? No, too touchy feely for me. I finally settled on something that I hoped would come across as friendly and professional.

My life then quickly became ruled by the flashing dot on my phone and the tell-tale flag notification which told me someone had liked my page and / or commented on something. It got ridiculous. I was out with Rob one evening having a lovely meal, phone on the table next to me. It was like I had developed a tick, every few minutes or so I would stealthily move my hand over towards my phone and just lift it up slightly so I could see if the little light was blinking, all the time trying to look like I was fully engaged in our conversation and thinking he couldn't see what I was up to when obviously he could. How rude! Even at night, I'd wake up to go to the loo and the light would be flashing and I just HAD to check it.

Crikey, when I got to 50 likes I was so chuffed. Then to 100, oh my gosh, that was amazing! And then people other than my friends started to like and comment on things. WOW! That felt incredible. It's funny how / where you get your confidence boosts and affirmations when you work alone. I didn't have a boss to tell me how I was doing so for me in those early days, I got my sense of worth in part from that page and the interaction with my followers.

If no one or very few people liked my post I would beat myself up about it, why? What was wrong with it? I found that when I posted something serious it got hardly any likes, but if I posted a picture of a cute dog I got more. Hmmmm. So, Facebook was about the feel-good factor, instant gratification. Ok I thought, I could do that.

So next I moved on to Instagram. I liked the idea of Instagram more than Facebook. It seemed a lot simpler and you could apply filters which made even my rudimentary photography skills look impressive. Again, I had the challenge of the logo fit so instead of messing about with it, I used a picture of me and Asha. It also seemed fitting to use a picture of her for my first Instagram post. The whole set-up was so much calmer and less arduous than Facebook had been. I breathed a huge sigh of relief.

A few months later I was out for drinks with friends and they had a friend staying with them who is basically an Instagram guru – he has around 55,000 followers. This guy makes a living from Instagram. Literally. Companies paid him to go to various places, overseas and in New Zealand, and take incredible pictures to promote their product. What a fantastic job!! So, over a few drinks I took the opportunity to have an impromptu social media lesson. He taught me a lot. He also did a post for me and the jump in followers and likes was remarkable. With my newfound knowledge and confidence, I went forth and insta-ed and hashtagged away!

I felt insanely excited one day when one of my posts was liked by a Real Housewife of Auckland, so excited in fact that I had to ring a friend who I knew would share my excitement, but I also knew they would laugh gently at me too. Soon after I had a head trainer / physiotherapist from a UK football club like a post and start following me. I'm not a football fan but even I had heard of his club and as per normal I rang a few friends to share my excitement and wonderment at the reach of social media. This like felt especially rewarding because like the affirmation I had received from the vet, it felt good to have a serious professional support me.

Just before Christmas I was sitting in bed catching up on some stuff on my phone when I flicked to my Instagram page. 289 followers. I want to get to 300 I thought.

"Hey Rob, how can I get to 300 followers? It would be a really cool way to start the new year."

"Hmmm. Have you posted that clip of Asha on the stand-up paddleboard with you yet?"

"No, I haven't. Is that really relevant do you think?"

"Why not? It's the holiday season and it's a cool little video. Go for it."

Boom. It worked. I posted just before I went to sleep and when I woke up in the morning, I had achieved my goal. I was SO happy.

Sitting at the kitchen table one summer Sunday evening, sipping a glass of wine and chatting to Rob I noticed a flurry of Instagram notifications on my phone. Wonder what that's about I mused. Clicking on an icon I saw that I had been tagged in a comment. I looked further and nearly wet myself. One of my clients who is quite famous in New Zealand had written a post on me and tagged me. That was great exposure and I needed to get onto it and comment. I tried to think of something appropriately witty to say. I came up blank. My client is so lovely, I really did want to thank her for posting about me. The number of followers I was getting on the back of just that one post was fantastic. In the end I settled for something relatively bland but professional (it's a business page I kept reminding myself) when what I really wanted to say was "I love you, thank you!"

I have been Snapchatted whilst massaging a couple of my clients, but so far that is still a mystery to me. I have a friend who is all over Twitter. She has a very important job and is truly responsible so makes thoughtful and inspiring tweets. Every time we have a conversation about it, I come away thinking, yeah great idea, I should do that. And then I sleep on it, wake up in the morning and think, yeah... nah. Don't think that's for me. I figure it is still just me after all and I have to draw the line somewhere.

The art of juggling

I can do this I thought to myself as I looked at my calendar. I had a fully booked day of clients and a 45-minute drive to the clinic where I would be for the day. It was 7.30am, I had packed my things for the day, and I needed to take Asha to the vet. The previous day I had noticed she was limping and looking uncomfortable and today she was booked in to be sedated as the vet suspected there was a grass seed that needed to be removed from her backside – there is a particular type of seed that comes from barley grass which has a nasty point and can penetrate into the skin of a dog and therefore needs to be extracted as soon as possible. Rob had already gone to work, and the plan was that I would drop her in and then he would pick her up later. All good I thought, I had plenty of time to get out of town and make my first appointment.

Asha knew something was up as she hadn't had a proper walk or her breakfast. I strapped on her harness and got her into the car, all the while making excited positive sounds which meant she probably thought she was going to some cool beach for a run.

Not the case. We arrived at the vet and everyone made a fuss of her. She loves it there as she always gets treats. Not this time.

Our vet Allison came out to greet us. "Are you ok for time because we thought you could stay while we do this as she's better with you there, and she's only having a mild sedative. Should take no more than an hour."

I looked at my watch, mentally making my journey calculations, that should be ok I thought. An hour and I'd still have time to get home, grab my stuff and get on the road.

"No problem," I said.

We all walked into the consult room where a little bed had been arranged on the floor. I could feel Asha hesitate at the door and I gave a gentle encouraging "come on gorgeous".

We settled ourselves around the bed, but Asha had well and truly tensed up. I did lots of deep breaths and sent her calming vibes. Allison came in and knelt in front of Asha, explaining to me that she was going to give her an injection to sedate her. The injection went in, Asha sat there. We gave it five minutes, but she was definitely not looking drowsy. Allison said she could give another one, she did, and we waited again. Another 10 minutes passed, and Asha was still showing absolutely no signs of sleeping.

Allison left the room and came back with a couple of nurses.

"This won't take long," she reassured me.

I held Asha while the nurses shaved a little patch on her foreleg where they could insert an intravenous catheter and from there administer some drugs that would finally knock her out.

We waited again.

Asha gradually started to go a bit limp and we lay her down.

Yes! I thought as I looked nervously at my watch, figuring I could still get to my clients on time.

There followed a lot of work on Asha's rear end with the vet trying to find the pesky grass seed.

"Ugh, what's that terrible smell?" I asked as a revolting aroma enveloped the room and nearly made me gag.

"Oh Asha," said Allison in a resigned voice, "she's just pooed on me." How embarrassing.

"She definitely went for a poo this morning," I said, embarrassed that my dog had pooed all over the vet.

"It happens all the time," said one of the vet nurses as Allison tried to take her poo-covered watch off.

I looked at my clean, poo-free watch. My timeframe was getting tighter and tighter and I could feel myself getting anxious. I had a couple of new clients that day and I really hated being late. Compounding my angst was the fact that I had left my phone in the reception area, and even if I could get to it, my file with phone numbers for my clients was at home in my work bag.

I couldn't leave my dog now anyway, nor would I have wanted to.

"I've nearly got it," said the vet as she concentrated harder. Phew I thought.

Finally, the procedure was finished, and it was time to give Asha some wake-up juice.

A bit like the sedation, Asha wasn't playing ball and although she lazily opened her eyes to gaze at me (which made me feel awful after what she'd just been through) she absolutely refused to move. I gently rocked her to try and initiate some movement, but she just flopped back down. She needed to at least be able to stand up before I would be allowed to take her home.

I wrapped my arms around her middle to see if I could help her to stand. Nope. Again, she just flopped down. By now I knew that I wouldn't make my first appointment and was stressing that I needed to get hold of my client to let her know before she left her own house to make the appointment.

It seemed like an eternity but finally Asha managed to get to her feet, so together with one of the nurses we bundled her up in a blanket and carried all 27kg of her out to the car. I promised to come back to pay the bill later and headed swiftly for home.

As I drove away my petrol light came on. Wonderful, that's all I need. I made a quick detour to the petrol station, forgetting that Asha, in the back seat, wasn't too stable and stopping at the pump a bit abruptly. Luckily, we have a hammock as a seat protector in the back seat, so Asha unceremoniously rolled from the back of the seat towards the front of the car, thankfully being caught and stopping mid-way, kind of wedged behind the seats and suspended by the hammock. I looked round at her and she looked back at me a bit startled. She was calm though and still stretched out along the length of the back seat.

I quickly filled up the car and headed home.

The next dilemma was how on earth I was going to get Asha into the house on my own. She was so floppy I didn't want to accidentally hurt her and being sedated she felt so much heavier than normal. I parked the car as close to the front door as I could and then by gently pushing and pulling her, I managed to manoeuvre her into a position where I could gather her up off the back seat. Lifting her out of the car in her blanket and carrying her into the house, all the while trying not to drop her or trip on her blanket, we made it inside.

Finally, I was able to ring my first client and ask whether she could meet me an hour later. She was so nice about it and even asked if I wanted to reschedule her dog's session for another day. I brushed off the suggestion, "No, no, it's fine, I'll be there by then for sure."

I set up Asha in the study. She was extremely wobbly from the sedatives and not steady on her feet. I was a bit worried she could fall and hurt herself if I left her alone. I realised I wouldn't be able to leave her and that my hastily rearranged appointment might have to be cancelled after all. I tried calling Rob to see if he would be able to help. No answer. Must be in a meeting. I considered whether I could take Asha with me and leave her in the car but discounted that idea pretty quickly as it would add to her stress. I tried a million more times to reach Rob and finally he answered.

I explained what had been happening over the last few hours and asked hopefully, "I don't suppose there is any chance at all that you could get home to look after Asha and work from here?"

Bless him, he agreed but said he couldn't be home for another hour.

I was still watching Asha as she drunkenly navigated the room. I tried to think of my friends who might be around at this time on a Wednesday morning. There was only one I could think of who might be around, so I gave her a call.

She didn't like dogs all that much, so I knew what I was asking was a bit of a tall order.

"Seriously, she won't be any trouble. She'll probably just sleep. I just don't want to leave her on her own." I explained. "And by the time you get here Rob will be back in 30 minutes."

"Will she bark at me?" asked my friend. I looked at my dozy dog who was struggling to hold her head up properly. "It's very unlikely," I told her confidently.

Eventually that day I had a happy client, a happy friend and a happy dog, and reflected on the fact that so many people were prepared to help me.

Bailey

Mum, Mum, Mum," I screech down the phone.

"Oh, hello darling, I thought it might be you. How are you?"

"Mum, I've met the most gorgeous dog".

"Ooooh, let me turn the telly down a minute and switch the kettle off and then I'll be with you". I can hear her moving away from the phone and a faint 'I'm still here, I'm still here, nearly done' as she gets herself ready to talk. Picturing my mum moving from her lounge through the hallway to the kitchen, and back again makes me smile.

"Ok, go ahead," she says as she gets back in her comfortable chair.

"He's 14 and a half."

"Well that's a very good age."

"His name is Bailey."

"Oh yes, and what is he?"

"A golden Cocker Spaniel."

"Stop right there!" says my mum.

Oh dear. I'd forgotten how sensitive Mum is about Cocker Spaniels. When I was about six years old, I had woken up one morning to a very strange sound coming from downstairs. I collected my brother from his room and together we went to investigate. "What's that funny noise?" we asked our parents. It sounded like a sheep was downstairs. Mum had made us wait in their bedroom while she went downstairs. It was all a big surprise and I remember how excited my brother and I were. Suddenly, this delightful ball of black and white fur, all long ears and big feet came running into the room whimpering gently and jumping all over us. She was so soft, and my brother and I just gazed at each other in amazement. WOW! We had a dog! We called her Misty and she was the gentlest, most loving dog you could hope for. She would play chase with us around the house and was very tolerant with us. She lived to a ripe old age and I remember being utterly inconsolable when she died.

A year or two later my parents got another dog, Jess. This one was a golden Cocker Spaniel and she was the complete opposite of Misty. She was gorgeous, fluffy and gentle but her personality was not. Jess was a little savage. The sort of dog that when you are walking along the street and people would coo over her saying how gorgeous she is and then go to pat her and we'd be like, I wouldn't... seriously she was a bad-tempered little madam. She stole an ice cream once, straight out of a child's hand as he was walking along. We couldn't believe it; it was so embarrassing. We had to buy the poor kid a new ice cream.

While Jess was still young my mum decided to get another dog for her as company. Sam was a brown and white Cocker Spaniel and he was totally different to Jess and Misty. Sam walked into our kitchen trembling with fear and headed straight under the dining table, where he sat and shivered refusing to come out. Poor little thing. He was scared of everything when he was little, but he and Jess were firm friends. He was a gentle soul in contrast to her feistiness.

Back to Bailey.

Deirdre, Bailey's owner had found my details at their local dog day-care. He had compressed discs in his spine which had flared up recently and he was finding it hard to go from sitting to standing. His owners wanted to see if massage would help relieve his pain and make his life more comfortable. He was described as playful, silly, highly food motivated, cat obsessed and a lover of people, and Poodles.

Bailey had previously had acupuncture and responded well so I was hopeful that he would be a good candidate for massage.

I couldn't have been more wrong! When I first arrived, he was super-excited, very happy to see me, vying for attention. The moment I tried to do my massage work, Bailey was having none of it. He shied away, panting and whining, drinking water and circling the room. Every time I started to touch him it was like the touch made him go a little crazy. He couldn't stand it. It wasn't from pain; it was over-excitement combined with concern that it could hurt him. Great. With a combination of wonderment and confusion we all sat watching Bailey. I thought back to my time in Chicago and decided to spend some time on trust building and energy work instead. I then showed his owners some techniques they could do with him in the evenings to try and reduce his excitement.

I was hopeful that our next session would be more productive as Bailey wouldn't be meeting me for the first time and, with any luck, he would understand that I wasn't there to hurt him.

Nope, not a chance. Session two was a repeat of the same shenanigans with only marginally more time actually spent doing some productive massage. A couple of sessions later and we had an idea. We had found that if we had some food it would distract him, but he got through way too many treats than was healthy, so we tried a Kong toy with one of his biscuits stuffed inside. Eureka! That worked. Thank goodness!

From that moment on Bailey's extremely patient and caring owner would make up a mash of sweet potato and biscuits and sit calmly on the floor holding the toy filled with this mixture and Bailey would receive his massage. He could get through a lot of sweet potato too for a little dog.

After about a year his family moved to a different city where he lived out his days in comfort.

15 minutes of fame

All publicity is good publicity. Well that's what they say isn't it, so it must be true. Well I'll let you into a little secret – it's not!

"You need to send out a press release," says my marketing guru friend Merran. A what? Yes of course I'd heard of press releases, but I'd never thought that it would be something I'd have to do. I was doing canine massage for goodness sake, not negotiating a trade treaty.

"It'll be great coverage, you'll get your name out there, it's a chance to pick up clients and you're the only one doing it in Auckland so they'll love it, it's a great story," she says.

So, I draft a press release, email it to my friend for her to review and polish, and then I boldly send it out to a couple of magazines and a TV show.

O H M Y G O D. A prime-time TV show called Seven Sharp responds almost immediately and wants to talk to me. I'm sitting at my desk at home and I start manically flapping my hands and hyperventilating at the same time.

"What's happened? What's the matter?" Rob rushes in. Even Asha has roused herself from the chair in the corner and is looking curiously at all the commotion.

I literally can't get my words out, so I just gesture at the screen in front of me.

Rob peers over my shoulder and reads the email.

"That's great babe!"

I still can't speak.

I message my friend and ask her what she reckons – "Awesome! Go for it".

I've never actually watched the programme, so I then ring another friend of mine and ask him what he thinks of the show. He's not the most complimentary but he tells me to prepare and it will all be ok.

The journalist and I go back and forwards over email, trying to arrange dates for filming. I've told everyone I know by now that I'm going to be on telly. Finally, I think, my dad will be able to tell his friends how proud of me he is – I'm no longer simply the daughter who moved to New Zealand, quit her fabulous job and now massages dogs for a living. I'm going to be famous! I start panicking about the inevitable influx of clients this is going to mean for me. I've only been open for business a couple of months, so this will be incredible.

One of my friends is a bit of a veteran at public appearances. She's been on TV many times, so I call on her for some tips in dealing with my upcoming moment of madness. She comes up trumps, as I knew she would, and gets me in front of her PR advisor who spends a good couple of hours prepping me for my appearance. Thank goodness for my friends. I truly can't imagine where I would be without them.

I have a chat with the journalist over the phone and he sounds ok. I ask him what his angle is going to be, whether there are some areas I should focus on and he is predictably vague. So, I just prepare myself to the best of my ability. Again, Rob comes home and the kitchen and living room are covered in multicoloured flip chart mind maps. I have my core statement and my key messages. I've decided my angle – serious with a hint of humour, and I keep practising to anyone who will listen. In the meantime, I google the journalist. What I find is a mix of pieces, some I enjoyed watching, some I didn't. It gave me no insight as to how he would be playing it with me. I reasoned though that it was national TV, so surely it would be good.

My next dilemma was what on earth to wear. I mean – this is national TV we're talking about and something I want to be able to look back on with pride and not think that I look unstylish. Vain I know but hey, it's important to me. So, one afternoon I pull everything out of my wardrobe and try and cobble together something that I can wear to the park. The work thing is easy because I'll wear my normal uniform (black or grey t-shirt and black or grey pants with trainers) but the journalist had asked that we go somewhere nearby for some "outdoors" filming with me and Asha. When Rob got home from work, he was subjected to several outfit possibilities, me turning my back to him and bending over "is it ok like this too?" To his eternal credit he didn't laugh at me and was extremely patient with my multitude of outfit changes. Eventually after a couple of hours and some glasses of chardonnay we landed on a suitable outfit, and I sent pictures of it to Debbie in the UK and my sister-in-law in Perth to get their ok. All good. Next, I panicked about the amount of makeup I should wear so dedicated some serious bathroom time to sorting that out. Finally, I arranged to get a haircut and eyebrow shape (I said I was vain!).

The day of filming arrives and it's a beautiful autumn day, sunny, no wind or rain and I wake at the crack of dawn full of nerves. The journalist is on a flight from Wellington, so I've got a few hours before he is likely to arrive. I've cleaned the house; Asha has been bathed (much to her disgust) and I am ready. My friend, Daren, kindly offered to hang out with me for the day and be my driver. The journalist had asked that I organise a couple of clients to do live demos with, so I've organised three who are spread out across town.

Daren and I are sitting having coffee when Asha starts barking loudly, which means someone is at the gate. I take a huge deep breath and approach the front door. Standing in front of me is a skinny looking guy wearing a shiny blue suit with a narrow tie, white shirt and polished black shoes (Oh I do hope the park isn't muddy). He looks a bit nervous and his eyes are darting behind me to where Asha's barking is coming from.

"Hi, you're ok with dogs, aren't you?" I ask dubiously. Surely they wouldn't have sent someone who was scared of dogs to interview a dog massage therapist.

"Yeah, sure," he mutters. I'm not convinced.

He walks through to the kitchen and Asha promptly runs towards him trying to get close enough to sniff him properly. He looks terrified. What a great start I think to myself.

Next comes the cameraman and again Asha is on full alert, suspicious of the massive bags he is carrying, and keen to defend her territory. He seems nice enough though and is very relaxed about Asha.

Both my guests have a poke around the house talking about where is the best place to take shots. Daren and I hover around expectantly.

"Is there a park or somewhere near here we could go with your dog?" asks the shiny-suited one. Thankfully there is a nice park overlooking the sea a short stroll away.

They wire me up with a microphone and we all head off down the road.

"I think he's afraid of dogs," I confide to Daren as we are walking behind the TV guys. "That's a bit ridiculous." Daren motions at my microphone. Oops, I've probably already managed to offend him. Brilliant way to start the session.

A walk that normally takes all of five minutes, takes what feels like an absolute age but we finally arrive at the park.

"Can you just do some stuff with the dog and we'll take some film and get set up," the journalist asks. Asha is in heaven; this is her second walk of the day and it's to one of her most favourite parks in the whole wide world. As it's about 10am on a Friday there is no one else around for which I am eternally thankful.

I chuck a stick a few times for Asha, all the while trying not to look like a fool – does my bum look big in this is the thought that keeps on churning round my head. Daren stands on the sidelines giving me encouraging nods.

Eventually the journalist and cameraman are ready and so he starts the interview. I've never done anything like this before and it's a bit weird. We do several 'takes' where I repeat myself and the journalist moves around trying to get different angles. I get the impression that's more about him than me. Over and over I repeat myself, focusing on my breathing and trying to relax and smile. I say a silent thank you to my friend Abbie for setting me up with her PR friend for my media training. Trying to answer his questions I'm also wondering what Asha is up to but don't want to move my head too much otherwise we'll have to do it AGAIN! After what feels like a whole morning but is probably only about 30 minutes, we are done so it's time to wander back home.

I hadn't for a minute thought they would want to do anything at home, but the journalist says he wants to do a bit with me at my desk. So, we try and sort that out and to be honest it makes me feel even more silly than I felt at the park. It's all just so staged – he even dragged out the fake dog skeleton that I'd bought when I returned from Chicago to help with learning the anatomy and physiology of the dog and balanced it precariously on the side of the desk.

With that done he seems content to go and see the clients I've arranged to work on. First is Aggie who's a Blue Heeler. She is incredibly obliging and lovely and calm despite the two strange men with their equipment in her living room. The journalist sits on the sofa and asks questions about what I'm doing and asks Aggie's owner Rhona a few things. At one point he leaned right over and got right in Aggie's face – Rhona and I held our breath – I don't know many dogs who would be comfortable with that and it confirms to me that he is most definitely not a dog person.

Next comes Indy, a beautiful, slightly nervous Ridgeback cross. Again, Indy is very obliging however she's rather scared of the camera. Her owner Kelly is amazing and talks to the journalist like a professional, singing my praises and the benefits of massage. Yes!

Finally, we have gorgeous Mischa, an elderly German Shepherd. We can hear her little sister barking in another room and the journalist perches on the end of the arm of the sofa, as far back as he can possibly get, looking positively terrified. Mischa's owner Mark is brilliant and wears a 'Paw Justice' t-shirt so I really hope that gets in the shot.

On the way to each client Daren has been my chauffeur and general calming influence. I've had all my preparation work in the car, so I've been able to check my key messages before each session. Then finally the day is over and once the journalist and cameraman have gone it's time to buy my team of supporters a well-deserved drink.

I'd love to say that I enjoyed the experience, and I guess I did to a degree, but overall I was just pleased that I had stayed on point and not been distracted or lured into saying anything dumb. All I need to do now is put it out of my mind – easier said than done!

A few weeks later I had a message from a friend while I was out walking with Rob and Asha to say they knew someone in production who had said that my piece would go to air that night. PANIC. I take some deep breaths and try and calm my instant breakout of nerves. I draft a note to go out on my Facebook page, telling people to watch that evening.

The evening comes and goes and we're not on. I feel like a bit of a fool.

About a week later, I get a phone call from the journalist telling me it's going to be on. Learning from past mistakes I decide not to post about it this time and wait and see if it actually happens. I happened to have a client the night it was on, which was great as it kept my mind off it. The TV was on in the background so I heard a bit of my piece but didn't watch it. On my drive home I rang Rob to ask him what he'd thought – he was supportive but there was something in his tone that I took as a bit of a warning. I got home and watched it and felt completely crestfallen. The journalist had tried to turn my serious business into a pampered posh pooches puff piece instead of the rehabilitation and improved lifestyle service that it really was. What a jerk. Even worse than the journalist was the presenter of the show who dismissed my business as a folly and then to cap it off he said I was based in a totally different city. Idiot. The clue is in the name – AUCKLAND Canine Massage. As cross as I was, I figured people will take it seriously if it appeals to them, and now a whole lot of people knew about my business. I was also heartened to see several supportive comments on the programme's Facebook page, both from friends and strangers, slamming the presenter and the journalist for trying to turn a serious piece into a joke.

I guess only time would tell whether this publicity was good publicity.

Blog excerpt from Monday, 2 March 2015

Meet Mischa...

Mischa is a beautiful 11-and-a-half-year-old female German Shepherd. She has an extremely gentle nature and is very friendly towards both people and dogs. Each time I visit Mischa she runs to greet me, face smiling and normally showing off a toy. She will sassily push her younger sister out of the way for a pat.

Sadly, when Mischa was eight and a half she was diagnosed with arthritis in her hips. Arthritis is a common ailment in general for larger dogs as they get older, and even more so unfortunately for breeds like German Shepherds. Since her diagnosis Mischa takes a fish oil supplement to help keep her joints in the best condition possible. In order to minimise the impact of exercise on her

joints she has also had hydrotherapy regularly for the last few years.
Hydrotherapy is an excellent way to exercise dogs as it reduces the impact of exercise on their joints. Mischa now goes on the underwater treadmill which encourages her to use her back legs in a stress-free way.
She also still goes for normal walks… but takes her own time on these.

I have been providing therapeutic massage for Mischa since January to help relieve some of her arthritic pain. At first, she panted A LOT – telling me she wasn't quite sure about what I was doing. But we took it very slowly and I spent a lot of time working her ears and neck to help calm her. Now, whilst she normally pants at the start, she relaxes and calms more quickly.
After that first session her owners reported an increase in appetite and an improvement in spirits with her wanting to play. Since then they report that she seems better for a good few days following her massage.

Massage is important not only to help relieve the pain in her back legs, but also to help keep the tissues around her front as healthy as possible as she front loads quite a lot when walking. On average dogs carry 60% of their weight through their front so imagine how those front limbs are working if they have to compensate for carrying more!

People and their dogs

Transitioning from a job where I was part of a team and worked 100% with people, to a job where I worked on my own, largely at home with just Asha for company, was a bit of a culture shock to say the least. It was a part of my career change that I had given little or no thought to. I'd been able to work from home on occasion in my old job, so I just figured it would be the same. Wrong. In the early days I found it hard to motivate myself. I would find myself whiling away hours of time just surfing the internet. I didn't really understand it – I was doing something I absolutely loved and yet couldn't focus and get on with things. Until I had a deadline. Then I properly moved myself. But I found the lack of interaction with team-mates, and people in general one of the hardest parts.

Having spent all day at home, Rob would get in from work and the moment he crossed the threshold I would unleash a day's worth of conversation at him. I think it's what they call cabin fever and I found myself suffering from it on a regular basis. At the start, my focus was obviously on building up my business. I would set myself targets, who I needed to talk to, things I needed to research, and I would plan outings to break up the days – to vet clinics, to do chores, and coffees with new contacts.

Gradually my client base started to build up and as I got out more there was more interaction with people. It was hard though because during a massage session, the focus needs to be on the dogs not on me! I couldn't 'download' to my clients like I would a team member in my old role. I had to learn the art of restraint and simply listen.

I also found it extremely hard when I visited a client and saw they were doing things that really didn't help their animals, albeit well-meaning. I remember one client I started seeing shortly after I had officially opened for business and I would do home visits. The owners of this divine Weimaraner were really lovely people who loved their dog and provided him with the best care. Like many dogs I have seen over the years he suffered from hip dysplasia and was very sore, especially after a day at day-care. The house had carpeted stairs from the front door that opened to a beautiful open living area with shiny wooden floors. This was like an ice rink for the dog. There were no rugs or mats and the dog would chase his toy across the floor, legs splaying out in different directions until he came to an abrupt stop at the top of the stairs. These people paid for regular joint injections, specialist care and now massage, and yet with the best will in the world, those slippery floors were probably undoing most of the good work.

I also saw some rather odd practices.

After a session at another clients house the owner went into the kitchen and came back with a block of Cadbury's Dairy Milk chocolate.

"Wow that's a big block, you must need some energy," I remarked.

"Oh, it's not for me, it's for her," he gestured at his dog still lying dozily on my mat.

"Sorry?"

"It's her treat," he said, as if it was the most normal thing in the world.

"You know chocolate is toxic for dogs right?" I said somewhat incredulously. I mean this client was a bright guy, he would surely know that.

"Yeah, like alcohol is to us but we still drink."

Nothing. There was absolutely nothing I could say to that. I just watched disbelievingly as he fed a couple of squares of this chocolate to his dog.

Often my [human] clients would use the session as a bit of a therapy session themselves. That's natural I suppose. They are stuck in a room with me and their dog for up to an hour. If there is something on their minds then it's easy enough to mull it over out loud with me.

I had a bit of a scare when one client arrived on the doorstep of my clinic looking extremely pale, dog lead hanging in one hand with her other hand clutching her opposite shoulder.

"Oh my god are you ok?" I asked.

"I'm actually not too sure."

"What's happened? You look very pale," I said as I took the dog from her and ushered her gently down the hallway to take a seat in the room.

"I've either pulled a muscle or I'm having a heart attack."

Whaaaaaaat?

"Do you think I should call someone for you? An ambulance maybe?"

"No no, I'll just sit here, you massage him, I should be all right. I'll go to the doctor on my way home I think."

"If you're sure...?"

"Yes dear, you carry on."

She is a gorgeous client and one I have great conversations with but that particular session I tried to focus on her dog whilst keeping one eye on her and watching her every move in case she deteriorated. I messaged her later to find out how she was. She hadn't gone to the doctor on her way home but promised she would the next day. It turned out she had wrenched her shoulder lifting something from a high cupboard, thankfully.

Another vet friend of mine asked me to work on her elderly Chihuahua who was getting increasingly stiff and had numerous slipped discs. I was a bit nervous when I first started to work on him. At that point I didn't really know this vet that well. I knew she was a believer in complementary therapy as she had been supportive of my work in the past, however I was still a bit nervous. The first session I had with her dog was an impromptu one on the floor behind the reception desk where I just had a good feel of his little body and also got my friend to show me what she had been doing as she said she tried to regularly give him a bit of a rub and a stretch. Let me try and paint you the picture...

On some shelving behind the reception area is a smallish dog bed, in which, sleeping curled up tightly so it's hard to see where one ends and another starts, are two Chihuahuas. A cuter image would be hard to find.

Suddenly, a hand swoops in and gently lifts the little grey one out. He is lovely and warm and looks around in a bit of a daze, tongue lolling gently out of one side of his mouth. His owner whispers and coos at him as he starts to wake up. He is placed gently on the floor where he shifts his weight to get his balance and does a deep back stretch like an angry cat pose in yoga. Now his brother peeps over the side of the bed, to see what's going on.

All three of us sit on the floor and the owner shows me how she's been working on him. She lifts him gently until he is lying on his back between her legs, head resting on her tummy. She then stretches and works his muscles.

I can't help it, I wince.

She looks at me, "Whaaat?"

"Well, it's just that that pressure looks a bit strong for him."

"Really?" She looks surprised.

"Yeah," I nod and take him from her. "You need to warm the muscles up a bit before you can go in too deep," I explain. "Imagine how we react when someone puts their thumb straight into our tight muscle area." I look for her agreement.

"Yeah right it hurts," she says.

"Sure does," I agree.

"So, I'm doing it too hard?"

"Yes, you need to warm up the muscle gently first…" We sit on the floor together and I show her how to soften her pressure.

I try to explain as gently as I can.

"What you're saying is I nearly broke my dog!" she laughs sheepishly.

We agree a time the following week when I'm going to work on him. I arrive and carry him off to the treatment room I can use, wrapped in a fleecy blanket. It's winter so the room is a bit chilly and I want to make sure he's ok. I put him down on the mat and he immediately starts to shake. I talk to him softly in the hope that he will relax – it's a strange room and I'm still a stranger to him so I understand it will take a little while. Fifteen minutes later and he's still shaking mildly, and I've now wrapped him up in the fleece and am holding him in my lap. His owner comes in and sits down with me.

"I can't stop him shaking," I explain.

She reached over and feels the tips of his ears.

"He's cold," she says.

"Really? I'm so sorry, I thought I'd wrapped him up warm!"

I felt absolutely dreadful and pulled the fleece further around his body and ears. It's not the easiest thing trying to massage a dog that is wrapped up in a fleece. We decide that the room I'm using just isn't warm enough for this dear little fellow so future sessions are conducted in a room where the heating is nice and high. After each session, once I've put him back on the floor, he does a fantastic stretch and a good shake before he totters back to his warm cosy bed and cuddles with his brother.

PART 3

Hitting my stride

Asha in her happy place

An urban country fair

A aargh!" I grumbled frustratedly into the darkness.

"What what what?" mumbled Rob in a slightly panicked voice as he sat bolt upright, trying to rouse himself from a deep sleep.

"What was I thinking? What if no one wants to give their dog a massage, and those that do have psycho dogs and I look like a fraud?"

"You won't babe, it'll be fine," Rob muttered as he rolled over, "Now get some sleep, it's 3.20am!"

I lay there gazing at the ceiling with my mind racing a million miles an hour, negative thoughts going round and round. There were no signs of it calming down, so I took a couple of drops of my natural sleep remedy and tried to quieten my mind.

I must have fallen asleep eventually because the next thing I knew a truck sounded like it was reversing into our bedroom and it was time to get up. The day of the urban country fair at Asha's doggy day-care had arrived. It was a great opportunity for local dog businesses to exhibit their wares, and especially with Asha being a day-care dog, when I'd received the invite there was no way I was going to miss the chance to attend.

I leapt out of bed and marched straight into the office where I looked down at my extensive to-do list. Asha followed me and stood on the threshold doing her morning stretches.

"Sorry Ginger, I'm not going to be able to walk you this morning, but I promise I'll make it up to you later," I murmured to her as I stroked her head.

First things first I started to gather everything I needed into one place on the kitchen table, and then put the kettle on for some coffee. Rob came through scratching his head and yawning.

"Morning you," he smiled, "Let me know what you need me to do."

"Ok, well I'm just getting everything together. This is my list, but my problem is still how to anchor my sign to the stall. It would be great if you could help me with that."

"Sure. Remind me again what the set-up is like."

I grabbed a pen and drew a basic bird's-eye view of where I wanted to put everything. "The stall itself is three metres by three metres and I just need something at the front against the table to stand this on so people can see it. The weather looks great, so we don't need to worry about rain or wind or anything, and I've got my flag to put on the other side and my banner to hang in front."

I looked outside as I was talking, the weather looked great. Not too hot, some cloud cover and no wind. Pretty perfect really.

"Ok, I'll go under the house and see what we've got".

I ran over timings in my head as I gave Asha her breakfast. It was going to be tight, but I should be able to make it.

I continued corralling all my Auckland Canine Massage paraphernalia into the hallway and then went downstairs to see what Rob was up to. He was crouched under the carport surrounded by all sorts of pieces of wood, rope, string and tape, trying to work out how to anchor my sign to the stall. In the end we just threw the lot into the boot of his car and decided to improvise when we got there.

We drove down the road in convoy, leaving the Ginger One at home with a chew, and stopped at our favourite coffee shop around the corner for take away. I normally only drink decaf but I figured today real coffee would be good. I still had butterflies following my wakeful night and just needed to be able to focus. Again, we set off in convoy for the 10-minute journey and I could feel the coffee starting to do its work.

Arriving at the day-care centre in central Auckland was a sight to behold. The carpark had been transformed into a true urban country scene, complete with bunting, stalls, banners and hay bales. There were a few other vendors already there setting up as Rob and I walked over to our stall.

I couldn't have the dogs – or their humans – sitting on the cold tarmac and getting covered in leaves and tree debris, so we tracked down a brush and got to work.

Rob started to string up my banner at the back of the stall while I set up the inside. I had borrowed a couple of collapsible picnic tables from a friend so I set one up at the back of the stall with a poster, some flyers and the treat jar – you can't forget the treat jar! I had a cover for the table at the front which we weighted down. Years and years ago

Mum had given me some funky little tablecloth weights, essentially, they are weighted clips shaped like miniature garden tools that you attach onto the corners of the cloth to stop it blowing away. They have come in so handy over the years so again, we tied the cloth down safe in the knowledge that it would be secure.

Next job was to attach the sign at the front of the stall. A couple of days before I had done a full assault on the local hardware store and grabbed anything and everything that I thought we might need to secure this sign. We used the Velcro stickers to stick the pieces of wood onto the tablecloth which the sign would then be stuck to. Rob also got out his trusty cable ties to secure another piece of wood underneath the table.

One thing about Rob is that he is the king of cable ties! We have a tube of various sized ties that lives permanently in a drawer in the office, just in case the need arises, and a cable tie is called for. One time I got home from work and found Rob ferreting underneath my desk. When I had a look to see what he was doing, he was cable tying all the leads together. It looked like an extract from one of those giant hard drives you see in the films with wires and cables grouped together running the length of the floor / up the wall. His motto is 'If in doubt, cable tie it'.

We finished the velcro'ing and cable tying and stood back to admire our handywork.

"Noooo! It's upside down," I panicked as I looked at my precious sign that no one could read.

We quickly dismantled it, turned it up the right way and taped it onto the table top. We again stood back to admire our handywork, thankfully the right way up this time, and with the crisis over I finally looked around at all the other stalls.

The whole place looked amazing. There was a doggy treat stall selling home-made treats; a stall for the local vet with a gift basket up for raffle; doggy clothing and bedding stalls; a healthy dog food stall; dog treat boxes with their very own home-made 'doggy beer' available; human cakes and street food were on offer as well as a coffee cart. All the stalls looked inviting and there were even a couple of dogs already enjoying the vibe. Pride of place and framed by hay bales at the entrance to the carpark, was the day-care centre's new school bus – a specially kitted out transit van with benches and seat belts inside for transporting dogs, and the most fantastic design on the outside so it looked like an old British school bus. The bus would be officially unveiled at the fair and bookings were being taken for a walk in the forest.

Everyone looked calm but busy and there was an air of excitement around the place. I was offering a five minute dog massage for a gold coin donation to charity, and I hoped that would attract interest.

Rob and I had barely finished setting up when it was time for the fair to be opened and people started arriving. Rob was wearing an Auckland Canine Massage cap as my t-shirts were too small for him, and he was stationed at the front of the stall to garner attention for the offer. We had a lovely fluffy dog mat inside and one of Asha's comfy memory foam beds for dog clients to sit on, and a chair for humans in the corner.

I watched as people travelled towards my stall, read the sign and moved on. Then came my first punter, a gorgeous six-year-old Spaniel/Poodle cross who was a bit uptight about everything that was going on. The five minutes flew by, I gave the dog a treat and the human a business card and Rob introduced me to my next client.

'Have you got me a t-shirt?' my friend Lynne asked from behind me as she arrived a couple of hours later to take over from Rob.

"I can't believe it's that time already!" I said. Wow, two hours had seriously flown by.

Lynne duly donned her branded t-shirt and positioned herself next to Rob to get his briefing. More and more people came by the stall and at one point I could see a little queue had formed. I looked at the donation jar – it was looking quite healthy.

One of my customers was a very stressed looking young Vizsla puppy. She was totally overwhelmed with everything; the smells, the people, the noise were all too much for her. She came and sat on the foam bed and let out a huge sigh. I gave her some treats but to start with she was just too stressed to eat any. I took lots of calming breaths and focused all my calming intentions on her and slowly she relaxed herself enough to take a treat before moving on with her owner.

After a few hours I needed a break and persuaded Lynne to hold the fort while I got myself something to eat and had a closer look at some of the stalls. There were more dogs waiting when I got back, and my friend Abbie had arrived to take over from Lynne. The sun had come as well and the whole fair had a lovely relaxed and happy vibe. I could see the other stall holders also doing great business.

"Can Daisy have a massage please?" asked a stall owner opposite me, pointing down at her dog. I recognised the dog from the morning, she had been sitting quietly next to her human and looked calm and relaxed.

"Of course she can!" I shouted back, aiming my voice between the people who had suddenly arrived.

Daisy came on over and had a blissful five minutes, she was so utterly relaxed and at the end of her time she simply refused to move. Abbie was busy taking photos of me and Daisy, who eventually had to move as the next customer was waiting.

All too soon the fair closed, and we started to pack up. I turned around to the entrance where I had heard a familiar bark and there was Rob with Asha straining at her harness to get to me. She had smelt my presence as soon as she got out of the car and she came bounding over once Rob allowed her to. One of her day-care friends ran over to Asha and the pair took off for an explore around the fair, hoovering up every little morsel of food that had been dropped on the floor. They had such a ball and whenever I looked over I could see Asha's smiling face and wiggling bottom manoeuvring around the empty stalls and people, rummaging in the hay bales. I didn't worry about her, she was quite safe there, I could see she had even managed to score a tumbler of doggy 'beer', so she was on good form. Once our stall was packed up it was time to head off, but Asha had other ideas. She had discovered the Mexican street food truck and was sitting patiently at the door to the truck, being fed leftover pieces of chicken. Uh oh.

"Hey you, I think you've had enough," I murmured to her.

She looked up at me, then back at the truck.

"Come on, off we go," I said, gently trying to guide her away. She refused to budge and continued to look imploringly at the truck owner.

"She's been very good," he said. "She just sat there so politely we couldn't resist." I smiled at my little monkey. On went her harness, we said our goodbyes and headed home.

By the time I fell onto the sofa I could barely talk, as all the adrenalin of the day deserted me. I had raised a decent amount for the Paw Justice charity from the massages I had given all day, and now a whole lot of new people knew about my business. A very successful day all in all.

The dreaded public speaking

In my previous career, at one of the companies I worked for in London, if I ever had to do any public speaking, I would bribe my colleague to do it for me. I hated it, passionately. My colleague used to do all the inductions for me, any training for new systems etc and she got some nice suppers out of that little deal.

As the years passed and I moved into bigger roles I couldn't avoid it any longer. I'm not entirely sure where the mentally paralysing, stomach churning, all over body trembling, complete and utter panic comes from when it comes to public speaking, but I know I'm not the only person who struggles with it. I guess looking back I did try to overcome it, but it was never something I volunteered to do. In fact, I even thought about resigning from a previous job just to get out of doing it. Friends suggested that something like Toastmasters might help, and I did go to one of their meetings once. Everyone was lovely but as I watched these fledgling presenters take to the microphone, I just knew it wasn't for me. So, I went to a hypnotist. She was amazing and the work she did certainly helped.

In one job I had in New Zealand I was told I would have to present at a senior managers' conference, and all the panic came flooding back. About an hour before the conference started, I did run wildly round the back roads of the town where the conference was being held with my mind racing, trying to think how I could get out of it. But I did it. A HUGE step. My manager at this company wasn't great in terms of her leadership ability but the one thing I will be forever grateful to her for is the course she sent me on to develop my presentation skills. Like most of my colleagues over the years she couldn't quite believe I had managed to get where I was while largely managing to avoid any kind of public speaking. So, she sent me on a two day presentation skills course. I nearly wet myself with fear but the lady who ran the course was incredible and over the two days we endured general humiliation in front of our colleagues as we were set tasks and filmed on our delivery. As sceptical as I was, it really worked and before I left the company, I managed to MC an event with a minimal amount of nerves.

All of this came in very handy when I was asked by a veterinary nursing college whether I would like to be a guest lecturer for them to talk about canine massage. I was absolutely delighted and more than a little chuffed to be asked and immediately replied that I would.

And then the nerves overtook me!

I had a whole two hours to fill on my specialist subject of canine massage. Now I love to talk about what I do but for that first presentation I was very worried that I would not be able to fill the time. While I have got better at presenting as I said, I'm not (and I seriously doubt whether I ever will be) one of those people who can simply stand up and talk with little or no preparation... and not look like a complete idiot. I had a boss once who could do that. He was amazing, and I was totally in awe of this skill of his.

"Helen Morphew, what am I talking to them about?" He asked me one time as we made our way to a presentation where he was opening the session. I looked at him aghast.

"Oh, I am so sorry, I thought you'd been briefed," I said.

"Well I can see what it says in the diary, but what do you want my message to be?"

"Right, ok, I think it should be..." I tell him as we get out of the lift and make our way to the auditorium.

"Ok, how long do I have?"

"You're on in about five minutes and you can talk for up to 15 minutes".

He went quiet for a while and I nervously watched him out of the corner of my eye to check he was ok. He seemed perfectly calm and not in the least bit rattled by the apparent lack of preparation. I would have been a basket case – no scrap that, it would never have happened to me because I would have practised those 15 minutes to within an inch of their lives. My incredible boss then got to his feet and calmly talked engagingly and impressively for 15 whole minutes. Something I couldn't ever imagine doing but hey who knows, I never thought I'd MC an event.

To prepare for the vet nurse talk I mapped out what I wanted to say and then pulled everything together in what I considered a rather impressive PowerPoint presentation. And I practised. I practised to Rob while the poor guy was trying to eat his supper in peace. I practised in the shower. I practised on Skype to my mum. I practised to Asha (yep, I did that!) and I practised to at least a couple of long-suffering friends when I'd invited them over for wine, only to receive an hour's talk from me.

I love canine massage, but I was worried that it might be a bit hard for the students without a real-life demo dog for me to work on. Asha would be hopeless. I'd tried using her at a very small informal chat I'd given at a vet clinic I was working at but she absolutely point blank refused to relax and would barely lie still for two minutes to allow me to demonstrate some techniques. So, Asha was a no.

I mentally ran through my clients and after rejecting a few; too nervous or too old to travel or too hyper I thought of the perfect pair. A friend owned the calmest most delightful two German Shepherds you would have ever met, and I knew they would be an instant hit with the students. As it was mid-week, I crossed my fingers that their owner would be able to make it and thankfully she could.

All sorted. I had the presentation written and I was happy with what I would say to support the notes and I now had my demo dogs.

The actual day of the lecture arrived, and I was predictably nervous as hell, but I used all my training to keep my nerves at bay. The dogs were a huge hit with the students, and I'd made sure that there would be some interaction with them through the talk to keep the students interested. Having the time slot after lunch is always tricky to keep people awake so I asked the class to do an exercise to get them practising on each other, which went something like…

Me: "Now what I need you to do is get into pairs, one of you sitting on a chair and the other one behind so we can do this together."

Them: Shifting nervously in their seats and glancing sideways at each other.

Me: "It doesn't matter who you partner with, just get into twos."

Them: A few brave souls start to pair up and they start chatting to each other and giggling.

Me: "I know, I know, I felt the same way when I was told I had to massage someone but come on, you're all fully clothed and it's the best way of learning this."

Them: More shuffling and the general chatter and giggling in the room escalates.

Me: "There's no need to make it weird!"

Them: Finally, they are paired up with a smattering of militants refusing to play ball. The energy at the room is at its peak.

Me: "Right, three deep breaths everyone."

Them: Copying my three deep breaths they calm down and we manage to get on with the presentation.

When it came to my demo dogs they were as good as gold. The whole room was quiet, students holding their breath and looking on curiously as I worked on one of the dogs. Normally she whinges and chats throughout her massage, but she must have sensed how important it was for me and she remained quiet and patiently allowed me to demonstrate various techniques on her.

Obviously both dogs and their owner were awarded cheeky little goody bags for their troubles. After that first lecture, I was on such a massive high. I couldn't believe I'd done it but boy was I tired by the time I got home. All that preparation, nervous energy and adrenalin meant I slept the best sleep I'd had in weeks.

Bobby

S o, what's this then?" the well-dressed man asked me as he walked up to my table at the doggy day-care where I was waiting to give information to interested pet parents.

"Well, it's massage for dogs," I replied. "Why?" he asked, "Why would they need it?"

"For the same reasons we do, it helps relieve pain, improves flexibility, reduces anxiety and promotes relaxation," I say. "Do you have massage?" I ask him. "God no," he says. "I hate people touching me."

"Ah, right. Well a lot of my clients are arthritic, and it helps them, also those recovering from surgery or an injury."

"Ok, I'd like my dog to have one."

"Excellent, what issues does he / she have?"

"None."

"Oh."

"Well you've just told me how good it is for them, so I want him to have one."

"Great. Ok then. No issues you say, nothing at all?"

"No. He's about six, he's in great condition but he'll love it."

So, we swap information and he asks me to get in touch with his wife, which I promise to do later in the week.

Two days later, I'm at the same stand at the same day-care and a lady walks up to me.

"My husband met you the other day and came home and told me he wants our dog to have a massage. I need a bloody massage, but he hasn't offered me one," she says. We both laugh.

A week later I arrive at Bobby's home for his massage session.

He is a beautiful golden Spaniel/Poodle cross with the longest eyelashes I have ever seen. He is soft and fluffy with impossibly long ears. He jumps up excitedly at me when I arrive and later as I sit at the kitchen table going through my intake form with his pet parent. Among the information I receive is the fact that Bobby jumps a lot, so I immediately assume that he will have tight hamstrings. While we talk about him, he lies on his cushion in the corner, watching what's going on.

When I sit on the floor and beckon him over, he comes straight over and lies down on the mat in front of me.

I start really gently and slowly, like I normally do to ensure that I don't move too quickly. As I start to work towards his hind legs he whips round and starts licking my hand. A sure sign that he isn't comfortable. So, I back it up, start working his neck and shoulders again, but his reaction has confirmed my assumption that he has tight hamstring muscles.

I start working towards his hind legs and lower spine again, this time a gentle growl is sent my way. I sit still and take some deep breaths.

I back off again, and slowly work up to another pass at his hind legs. This pattern continues for a few more minutes until he finally seems to understand that I'm not there to hurt him or inflict pain on him. I get the opportunity to start to work his hind leg and he tenses up immediately, but slowly starts to relax. While holding the muscle and gently working it he elicits some jump signs, so I know he's holding a fair bit of tension in his leg. Bless him, he gave a big sigh as he laid his head down gently and closed his eyes and let me work.

Whilst Bobby and I are having this little dance, his pet parent is also there, providing a comforting presence for him. She and I have a disjointed conversation going – the kind I guess you have when you have young kids, you know you start a sentence and then something distracts you and you pick up the conversation at a totally different part from where it left off, or a new topic.

"So," she asks, "how often do you think he needs one, every month?"

I look at her and smile.

"If you want to give him a massage every month then I'm sure he would love it," I say, "but he doesn't 'need' it. How about I make a note to get in contact in a couple of months and we could look at once a quarter maybe?"

Such completely gorgeous people.

Sending it out to the universe

One of the reasons I chose the course at the Chicago School of Canine Massage was because I hoped it would set me up to work credibly and professionally alongside the veterinary, animal rehabilitation and animal physiotherapy industries.

Very early on, I had decided that I would focus on building relationships with these professionals, and that I wanted to have three locations across Auckland that I could work from. That would mean three days at clinics, with home visits (and the dreaded administration work) on the other days. Being able to operate from a clinic as opposed to purely offering home visits was important for me. In a clinic I could control the space and it would therefore be a benign area with nothing for the dog to do other than relax. At home there were a myriad of distractions for a dog – the courier driver to name just one. I wanted to reserve home visits for those who were too mobility-challenged to travel.

My own vet was really supportive and cleared a smallish space in their clinic for me to work from. Over time a new room was set up which I shared with another therapist. This was a central-city location so worked perfectly for people living close by.

One down, two to go.

When I had been kicking my heels before going to Chicago, meeting various people and building my future network, I had met a very inspiring lady. Karynne lived and worked about 45 minutes from me and ran a canine hydrotherapy business. We clicked as soon as we met and she was extremely generous with her time, allowing me to watch a couple of her sessions when the dogs were on the underwater treadmill and in the pool. She seemed really switched on and the way she ran her business looked very professional. We caught up for coffee once I'd completed my training in Chicago, and I talked to her about how amazing it had been to visit a rehabilitation centre where there was hydrotherapy, physiotherapy, massage and chiropractic care all under one roof. The ultimate dog rehabilitation centre as I saw it. She totally agreed with me and explained that would be her ideal scenario too.

Fast forward a few months and I received a call from a rehabilitation vet, Steph, who I'd met a few times, asking whether I would be interested in leasing space from her out at the hydrotherapy centre. The plan was to build a cabin in the grounds of the existing hydrotherapy centre which would be used as a treatment room for rehabilitation. Would I be interested? Hell yes!

While it would mean a fairly long journey for me from home, it would mean that I would have a space in South

Auckland. Plus, I would be aligned with two other credible and professional businesses. I absolutely loved it. So pretty much every Wednesday I headed down to Patumahoe to see my clients in the cabin – a far cry from my urban home in Auckland's Westmere. Patumahoe is full of lush fields with farm animals grazing all around. The space itself seemed to have a calming effect on me, which in turn rubbed off on the dogs.

I looked forward to my Wednesdays at the cabin and especially enjoyed the sense of camaraderie I felt by working alongside these women. Finally, I could run thoughts and ideas past people who were operating in the same industry.

The opportunity then arose to purchase a boarding kennel facility that was close by, and it could be converted into the truly holistic therapy and rehabilitation centre we all dreamed about. I wasn't going to be financially invested but I was a HUGE supporter and advocate, and I remember when the deal was completed and we all stood around on the deck outside the old hydrotherapy place, champagne flowing, and I thought how lucky I was to have met these incredible women.

The move to this new base is now complete, as is the remodelling of the old kennels. The old cabin is in its new position, looking out over fields and trees. It has a separate entrance and a fully fenced area, with the cutest of hand painted-murals, so the dogs can be allowed safely off lead. There is a strip of sand along the back of the cabin for observing how the dogs carry their weight when they walk, and flowers planted along the fence line.

Inside the revamped kennels there is a brand-new state of the art underwater treadmill with options for walking on a gradient, a new pool has been built, the reception area is smart with colourful products available to buy, and the new kennels and run for dogs who are staying whilst undergoing rehab are ready for their four-legged visitors. The Southern K9 Therapy Centre feels calm, professional and welcoming.

We decided to hold a grand opening night for industry professionals, and the evening was a huge success. Lots of vets, physios and specialists arrive to check the place out. I feel incredibly proud to be part of the very first dedicated therapy centre for dogs in the whole of New Zealand.

As for me and my business ambitions, with central and south Auckland covered, I now needed to find a base on the North Shore.

Over our Christmas break one year, on a stunning summer's day, Rob and I decided to take Asha to a dog friendly beach near Castor Bay on the North Shore of Auckland. We took my car – the Auckland Canine Massage Mobile as it is now referred to – because Rob didn't really want a stinky wet dog in his car. We spent a couple of hours on the beach having fun before we packed up to head home.

As we got into the car, I noticed something under one of the windscreen wipers. On closer inspection it turned out to be a business card from a local vet and on the back was written "Call me to discuss a business proposal." What the heck?

Gotta love a branded car sometimes, I guess.

I rang the number, and we arranged to meet at her vet clinic. It was a lovely clean and professional space and I immediately warmed to Nicole. She had big plans for the practice, and showed me a room she wanted to turn into a therapy room. It was currently part of the cattery they had there, so it needed a fair bit of vision, but I told her I was definitely keen.

True to her promise, a couple of months later the room was transformed into a serene, welcoming and calming space for dogs. Like the other two clinic spaces it had a separate entrance so dogs who get anxious when they visit the vet would be ok. It even had a heat pump so would be warm in winter and cool in summer – Yuss!

Nicole explained that she would ideally like more than one therapist operating in the room, and as I could only commit to one day a week this arrangement would be perfect. Soon after I came on board, one of the animal physiotherapists who I knew and liked also signed on to share the therapy room. Excellent, another complementary team. Even though we don't work very closely together, it's great to know she will be there one day a week when I need to refer a client. The final addition to the team was an animal chiropractor, who also eventually rented space at the South Auckland clinic.

I'm so excited to now have three clinic options to be able to offer clients. It's more convenient for them and it helps spread the word. I guess 'sending it out to the universe' worked.

Occupational hazards

"I am so sorry, hold your breath, she's just farted," announced my client as I walked through the front door.

I had seen the little French Bulldog sitting on the bottom step of the stairs as I got to the front door and when I peered in and knocked on the glass, she had shot off the step to come to greet me at the door. This exertion of energy had obviously caused the fart. And it was a good one.

"I think she needs to go out for a poo before you start," continued my client.

I waited on the step while the dog was sent outside to do her business.

It's a bit of an occupational hazard – dog farts, and in order of offensiveness, poo, vomit, burps, hair, oh so much hair!

When I was growing up 'farts' were never mentioned. People didn't do them; dogs didn't do them. They just weren't spoken about. I can literally remember only one time where I witnessed a fart from one of my parents when I was growing up. Now I'm English, and I might be in danger of grossly over-generalising, but we Brits, we enjoy a bit of bottom humour. So, when I first experienced a dog fart from one of my clients, I had to stifle a silly schoolgirl giggle. That was in the early days. Now it is more than likely that both me and the client will laugh out loud.

I think the first time I really witnessed a dog fart was many years ago at a beautiful English country hotel with Debbie. There was a British film star there with their English Bulldog who was wandering around snuffling and grunting in true Bulldog style, when he went behind my chair and let out a corker. Thankfully it didn't smell, but it was impressively loud.

Asha is a shocker with them. It is quite normal to be sitting on the sofa in the evening when suddenly, a foul stench will reach you from one or other end of the couch. This has normally been pre-empted by an abrupt lift of the head followed by an exit from the sofa and a swish of the tail.

A particularly potent attack happened after Asha and I had been to visit a friend.

It was a beautiful sunny afternoon and we had arranged to go for a walk with a friend who owns a large piece of land on the outskirts of the city. There were several dogs already there, so we went for a lovely walk for an hour or so. The dogs loved it, especially Asha. After much leaping around, chasing each other through the forest and swimming together (or rather launching at each other) in the ponds we returned to the house to relax. The humans, i.e. me and my friend, enjoyed a nice cold beer while the dogs drank as much water as they could.

One of the dogs is a bit of a fussy eater and so is fed at various intervals through the day to make sure he gets the right amount of food. He's fed raw food, and Asha is not. When my friend brought the frozen lumps of salmon out to the table in the garden, we were immediately surrounded by six sets of earnest and imploring eyes. One of those sets were Asha's.

"Does it matter if she gets some?" asked my friend.

"I'm not sure," I say. "She's not given raw food."

"She'll be all right", says my friend as Asha delightedly ran off with a chunk of fish.

Oh well I thought to myself, what's the worst that can happen.

One piece may well have been ok, but Asha proceeded to beg for another piece, successfully, and then stole a piece from the fussy pooch who'd had enough by this stage.

I kept my eye on her and she seemed fine.

In the car on the way home, a horrible smell hit me. The car windows were open because it was a hot day, and as we were passing fields full of cows and horses, I assumed that was where the smell was coming from. As we hit the motorway, I closed the windows and turned on the air conditioning. We hadn't gone far when a horrible smell hit me again. This time we were overtaking a lorry which I assumed was a livestock truck and that was where the smell was coming from. I quickly shut off the vents and turned the air to circulate within the car. Twenty minutes later we had reached the Auckland harbour bridge and once again the smell hit me. This time we were over water, there wasn't a truck in sight, and I glanced over my shoulder to see Asha stretched out on the back seat. "Oh my god it's you, you filthy devil," I said as she gazed back at me innocently. I quickly opened the windows and flushed the car with exhaust fumes and fresh air.

Dog farts are quite simply par for the course. When a dog is relaxed, out comes a fart. Some are quiet, some are loud. Some are smelly, some aren't. The dogs will often stretch as a precursor and then exhale and let it out. The other day a dog rolled away from me with a grunt and then let rip. One client regularly apologises for feeding her dog something particularly odorous that she knows will make him fart. The same client has been known on occasion to headline the session by telling me her dog hadn't been for a poo that day. We know we are in for a treat when she says that!

Dog hair is my other nemesis. It really doesn't seem to matter if a dog has been groomed or brushed that morning by its owner, I will always be covered in hair. Some are worse than others. I have a brown Labrador client whose fine hair unfailingly makes its way into my eyes, into my mouth and up my nose. Part of the session is always spent with me frantically rubbing at my nose with the back of my hand to try and rid it of hair, while also trying desperately not to breathe it in.

My other favourites on the hair front are a pair of yellow Labrador brothers. So covered am I by the time I finish with them that I look like a walking Labrador myself. It's a wonder that they have any hair left on them by the end of their session. It's always good to go from their session to the supermarket – the looks I get!

Trying to settle the dogs can sometimes be a bit of a challenge, especially when a dog is having what can only be described as a sugar rush. A regular client of mine arrived for her dog's session and she had been in a bit of a hurry, trying to leave work on time to pick up her dog and come to see me. Her whole day had been filled with meetings and she'd barely had time to eat so she had grabbed a giant muesli bar from the petrol station on her way to me.

Her dog was normally restless at the start of her session and we would use treats at the start and then trail them off as she gradually calmed down. This particular session the dog was even more restless than normal – panting and larking around, rubbing her face along my massage mat with her bottom stuck up in the air. Both the owner and I were laughing at her behaviour.

"Crikey, she really is a bit excitable today," I exclaimed.

"Yes, she is isn't she," said the owner.

"Any idea why?"

"Umm, well, umm, yes, well she might have a bit of a sugar rush."

"A what?"

"A sugar rush."

"How?"

"Um, well, um I was eating this muesli bar in the car and I could feel her eyes boring into me and so I just had to give her some." She confessed whilst pulling the remainder of the bar from her pocket.

"How much exactly?"

"About half."

"Oh dear, she really is having a sugar rush," I agreed as I read the ingredients on the back of the remaining packet. Seriously the biggest muesli bar I'd ever seen, full of fruit and additives.

"I think we'd better abort this mission," I said and we both laughed.

National radio

One normal Thursday evening I had arranged to catch up with a couple of friends for a bite to eat at a funky bar in town before we went to a comedy show. I hadn't seen these friends for a while, so I was really looking forward to a fun night. As it was in town as well, I was pretty excited about the fact that I could dress up a little bit, get out of my ubiquitous tracksuit pants, branded t-shirt and trainers.

I was enjoying a delicious glass of chardonnay and sharing an interesting tapas style dish when I noticed an email had come through on my phone. I opened the email and my jaw must have fallen to the floor:

"Hi Helen, I was going to ring... still will... just thought a bit of a heads-up might be helpful, especially given this is to do with an upcoming spot on the radio, if indeed you are willing and able! I am a journalist/producer with Radio Live... the national talk radio network broadcast on

100.6FM in Auckland. We are now hosting Radio Live's evening show from eight to midnight with some changes to format... including a Special Guest Hour between 8pm and 9pm in which a slot is set aside for a specialist guest and theme. One of them being 'Your Pet'... a wide brief but all to do with our feathered or furry friends... and everything else in between! After hearing about your move into the canine massage business, I'm wondering if you would be up for coming in as her studio guest at the Radio Live HQ in Ponsonby in a couple of weeks, specifically the evening of Thursday 21st May... Fascinating stuff. Never knew there was such a thing. Of course, you... as guest... are most welcome to suggest any other topics you'd like to canvas. The presenter will introduce and host the session which will involve chat but also fielding calls from listeners, as talkback is an element of the evening show. You would have to be in at our Ponsonby studio by 8pm but will be out by 9pm... It's a golden opportunity to market and advertise… as well as enlighten, entertain and inform Radio Live's listeners. Trust you agree. Drop me a line when you like, let me know if you are keen... and I'll give you a ring after the weekend, see if this sounds like something worthwhile for you. We'd certainly love to have you in as one of our specialist guests. The actual on-air time is eaten into by the news bulletin, show introduction, ad breaks etc… so don't feel as if you are going to have to fill a whole hour. Not at all. If anything, I think you'll find the time flies by too fast!"

Having had my fingers burnt with the TV show a while ago I was a little uneasy about any media stuff. I looked at my friends sitting opposite me. "What do you reckon?" I asked as I handed my phone across the table to them.

"That's awesome," said one of them. "Karen is a fantastic radio host and that's a serious station."

"But it's live," I gasped at them.

"You'll be fine," they said together. "Tell her yes."

I tapped back a positive reply and then took an enormous sip from my glass of chardonnay. Oh dear, here we go again, I think.

Getting home that night I ran into the house to tell Rob my latest news. He was, as ever, completely supportive and assured me I'd be great. I messaged my Chicago course buddy and his reply was just what I needed.

"Fantastic... and all from your own lips. No one to criticise what YOU are doing."

I racked my brains about who I could speak to about radio, whether I knew anyone who had been on there. I realised that sadly I didn't have anyone in my circle who at that time had done radio, so I was on my own for this one.

I dug out the media guide I had been given by my friend the last time I had needed media guidance and found the piece pertaining to radio.

I looked at my diary for the next couple of weeks. I was pretty busy so was going to have to juggle some things in order to get enough preparation time in. I think it must stem from my fear of public speaking that I really can't wing things. I must prepare what I'm going to say or present to within an inch of its life otherwise I find it too stressful.

So, for the next couple of weeks the house was yet again turned into a maze of flip charts and coloured Post-it notes. I also made it my goal to listen to the show I would be on, to understand the format and the type of approach they would be most likely to take. Poor Rob, again he was subjected to listening to me repeatedly. I made him ask me random questions to check my answers and his patience was unfailing. "You're great babe, you know your stuff," he reiterated time and time again.

When it came to the day of the show, I had pretty much cleared my diary of appointments so I could spend the day composing myself. I suddenly got an adrenalin rush while I was doing my voice preparations (from the media guide) and started dancing around the lounge to Wham! Asha got very alarmed and jumped around with me, barking at me. Rob just sat patiently on the sofa, probably waiting for the crash. Which came as we pulled up to the studio in our car.

"I can't do it," I said to him, as he pulled into a parking space.

"Yes, you can," he said. "You've done your prep, it's normal to be nervous, but you've got this."

I looked at him, feeling a sick churning sensation in my stomach and sticky sweaty palms.

"I really don't think I can."

"Yes, you can." And with that he got out of the car and came around to get me out.

I put my legs out of the car and bent over the gutter, feeling ready to throw up. Panic, panic, panic. I took three deep breaths and got out. With Rob holding my sweaty hand we walked very slowly and gingerly to the entrance. Another couple of deep breaths, a mint in my mouth and we were in.

The inside appeared a bit dark with low lighting. The producer came out to greet us and ushered us into a waiting area outside the studio, which looked like a giant goldfish bowl. All I could see were computer screens, big earphones, microphones and that really cool sign that I only thought existed in films 'On Air'. The radio host was finishing off her segment before mine was due, so I could see her talking into the microphone. As it was evening, most people seemed to have gone home and the rest of the office was relatively quiet.

The host finished her piece and then came out to welcome us. I was still in a bit of a state of shock about being there and felt like I was having a kind of out of body experience where you feel like you're floating. The next thing I knew I was sitting in the giant goldfish bowl, an enormous microphone in front of my face, a dial with buttons by my right hand, massive headphones on and Rob was seated in the producer's room on my left. I could barely see the host because of all the screens between us.

I tried desperately not to think of my parents listening in the UK, or all my friends who I'd told about my appearance. I focused on the host and her questions. I could feel my mouth was dry and my words coming out sounded a bit 'sticky', but I forged on, forcing myself to remain calm. When it was time for the public to phone in, I started to feel my nerves kicking in again – who knew what they would ask. I needn't have worried; the callers were very sweet and before I knew it Rob and I were back out on the street. The time had truly flown by.

On the drive home I was madly texting my friends to get their opinions and then I Skyped my mum and dad to get their views. Overwhelmingly it seemed everyone thought I'd done a great job and it was a success.

Phew. I could feel my view of the media being ever so slightly restored, but I also couldn't help reflecting on the fact that I had just been on national radio, talking about canine massage. Me.

National news

I was looking through social media one morning when I noticed an article and video about a local animal chiropractor. It was a nice little article and having a video along with it was pretty cool. It had been posted by The NZ Herald – a national New Zealand newspaper.

So, I started wondering whether they would be interested in me and before I thought too much about it I had sent an email off to the journalist who had written the article, explaining that I liked the piece she'd done on the chiropractor, and would she be interested in doing one on me.

To my surprise I received a phone call confirming that she would.

Crikey! Here we go again.

Like the TV guy, she asked whether I could set up a client to work on so they could take some pictures and video. I immediately thought of the German Shepherds I had used as my demo dogs for the vet nurse talks, so I rang their owner and asked whether she'd be up for it. Thankfully she was, and we managed to schedule a day that worked in nicely for all of us.

Let the prep begin!

The house was yet again covered in flip charts with coloured pens and Post-it notes with my messages and talking points. All too soon the morning of the interview arrived and after a predictably restless night I arrived at my client's home nice and early, ready for the interview. I really hoped that this time the interviewer wouldn't be afraid of dogs.

Thankfully the journalist and cameraman seemed relaxed around the dogs and while the cameraman set up and started taking some photos of Ebony, one of the dogs, the journalist started asking me some questions. I tried to remember my core messages and repeated them at every opportunity. Once the cameraman was ready, we got Ebony in position and I started to work on her.

"So, could you do that thing where they lie on their backs and you massage their face?" asks the Cameraman.

"Do what?" I ask.

"You know, like you see on YouTube when the dog is all zoned out."

I threw him a withering look and explained that I am a therapeutic massage therapist and the people you see on YouTube doing that are normally the dog's owner. And can you imagine how I would even start to do that with a 35kg German Shepherd?

He looks suitably chastised.

Ebony was an absolute star, as I knew she would be. The camera is click click clicking in her face and she remains so calm that her mood transfers to me and we have a great session. Her owner and brother watch on while she acts like a paparazzi pro.

I really try and do my best to explain what I'm doing while I do it, I'm mid-sentence about something when the cameraman asks me to stop talking as you won't be able to hear what I'm saying on the video and it'll look weird. Great.

Often when I work on the dogs the owner will remark to me that it doesn't look like I am putting much pressure on. I always take my time to explain while it might look light, I am applying as much pressure as the dog will tolerate. I have this running through my mind as we are shooting the video and wondering whether it's going to look like I'm actually doing anything. I try and exaggerate my techniques a bit, in the hope that it will come across better.

The session comes to an end and the journalist confirms that she has everything she needs, she'll let me know when it's going to run – likely this weekend – we say our goodbyes and I breathe a huge sigh of relief. Is 11.30am too early for wine?

It's a public holiday at the weekend and it's the weekend that Rob is away on a sailing race. He does it every year so it's a girly weekend for me and Asha. I have lunch with some girlfriends on the Saturday and talk to them about what I'd been involved with during the week. They are delighted for me and excited to see the article. I had checked the news online that day and it wasn't there so I assumed that it would be the following day.

I woke early on the Sunday morning and immediately checked the news website. Nothing there yet, but no chance now of me going back to sleep. A couple of hours later (yes, I checked every 10 minutes) and bingo there it is. With slightly trembling hands I read the article and watched the video. Phew! It was a good article and the video has come out really well. I messaged Rob so that he could see it when he had a chance to look at his phone.

It didn't occur to me that it would be in the printed version of the paper as well, so when a friend messaged me later in the morning to tell me they are reading my piece, Asha and I leg it up to my local shop to get a copy. Both shops are sold out. I walk away a bit crestfallen, thinking about who I can get a copy from. I pop into a café to get a takeaway coffee and I notice that they have a copy of the newspaper.

"Oh my gosh, I'm in here apparently," I say to the owner as I leaf through to find my bit.

And there I am, a half page all about me! I nearly fall over, I'm so pleased.

The owner looks over my shoulder.

"Wow, that's great," she says.

"Yeah, I didn't expect it to be in the actual paper, I thought it was going to just be online, so I haven't got a copy."

"Take that one."

"Really, are you sure?"

"Absolutely, it's not every day you're in The Herald."

She won't let me pay for the paper or the coffee so I leave the little coffee shop a lot happier than when I went in.

Wandering home, I reflected on just how remarkable this was. A national newspaper had run a story on me. I'm so pleased for what it means for the dogs in Auckland – more awareness of the therapies out there for people with dogs in need.

Shelter work

Working at shelters for dogs has always been something dear to my heart. I'm not sure why exactly, but all those big pleading eyes really pull at my heart, and I truly admire the incredible work these people do.

Years ago, when I was living in London, I was quite near to the Battersea Dogs Home. One winter the home put out an appeal asking for people to donate blankets and sheets. I rallied round all my friends to get their unused blankets but when it came time to deliver our donations, I couldn't actually go into the building for fear of what I might see. Silly really, as it's not like I would have seen anything bad. So instead, I did a speedy drive by, parked on double yellows and literally dumped the blankets and ran.

A few years later when I got to New Zealand, I saw a human resources job advertised at one of the shelters. I immediately applied for it, desperate to be around dogs. I mentioned it to a colleague one day when we were walking to get some lunch.

"Why do you want to leave this job?" she asked me. I didn't really have a very good answer other than to say I loved the idea of working with dogs.

"But you love what you do here, and you're really good at it. Why don't you volunteer there for a while instead and see if that scratches the dog itch?"

Great suggestion, why hadn't I thought of that?

By that time, I had already sent in my CV for the role, so when I got called for an interview I went along. My colleague's words were stuck in the back of my mind though. Why hadn't I volunteered before, what was holding me back? Was it the time commitment or the thought of what I might see? I was also harbouring doubts that I wouldn't be able to leave without a dog, or three, and Rob and I weren't in a position to have a dog at that time. The interview itself was fine, made all the more fun for me because of the two Retrievers who were also in the office and constantly vying for my attention. As it turned out the job didn't really appeal to me and that must have come across in the interview as I wasn't offered the position.

That itch had been scratched though and so I put my big girl pants on and applied as a volunteer. I had to go in for an interview, I was so nervous! More nervous I think than for the permanent role. I had learnt all about their mission, values and the Five Freedoms of animal welfare in case I was asked. I needn't have worried, it was a gentle interview and afterwards I was accepted. After all I was only applying to be a volunteer.

Speed forward a few years and Rob and I finally bought a house which meant we could also finally get a dog. On my first shift as a volunteer after moving to our new house I met Asha. She was such a gentle little soul, so tiny being only a few months old, and she took my heart immediately. All she wanted to do was sit on my lap and snuggle.

"I have found our dog," I announced to Rob when I got home from the shift.

"Ok, tell me more," he said. This wasn't the first time I had come home saying I had fallen in love with a dog, but it was the first time I could do anything about it, so Rob looked interested, and a little nervous!

"She's about four months old, ginger, really floppy and so gentle. We have to have her; she is absolutely perfect." Rob didn't need much persuading and the following week we both went in to properly meet her. Again, she was just totally smoochy and not really interested in anything other than us. Rob fell in love instantly. Done. The following weekend we headed out to pick her up and stopped at a pet store on the way. We must have looked like kids in a sweetshop, we were both grinning from ear to ear and hopping from foot to foot as we loaded up with all the bits and pieces we would need including toys, lots of toys!

On the course in Chicago we had the opportunity to go to a couple of different shelters. In both places a room was provided for us. The five students, plus instructor, would work on the dogs. Mainly this involved building trust with the animals rather than any meaningful hands-on work. One of the shelter volunteers would bring a dog to us and we would spend a good while with them, observing their behaviour, and learning to build trust. I fell in love with one dog in particular. He was a big brindle boy and sadly had been at the shelter for a while. He was gorgeous, so handsome. I really did consider shipping him back with me, but thankfully common sense (and Rob) prevailed and I came home from Chicago without any extra hounds. It was a great experience working with the shelter dogs, and it was after all in such a situation that I had discovered canine massage existed.

I bided my time and waited for an opportunity to use my canine massage skills at my local shelter in Auckland. Finally, it came. My roster supervisor sent an email asking if anyone was able to commit to any more shifts to help with handling a rather sudden influx of dogs. Being self-employed and building the business I could have fitted it in however what I really wanted was to be able to use massage in the shelter. There were a couple of dogs in particular that had been mentioned in the press that I knew would benefit so I put my business hat back on and drew up a proposal and sent it in to my supervisor. Thankfully I didn't have to wait long for a response. I was a bit nervous, what if they said thanks but no? I wasn't sure what I would do if that happened. I needn't have worried; I got the loveliest email back saying the head vet was supportive and they would love it if I could come in to work on these dogs.

Now I can be a bit emotional at times, particularly when it comes to any kind of perceived suffering or sadness to do with animals, so I was concerned about whether I would be able to hold it together. It was fine. I was professional, everyone was lovely, and the dogs were so gorgeous. The following week when I went back in, I got positive feedback from one of the staff members, saying that she noticed a difference after their last session. I was so pleased I'm pretty sure I started to tear up

Don't get me wrong, I still regularly want to bring dogs home, but so far Asha is an only dog. The dogs are very well cared for and regardless of how they have ended up in the shelter, if what I do can provide a bit of relief that is all I care about. I liken it to when I first got to Chicago when I was anxious, didn't want to eat and generally felt homesick. Now I'm not saying that dogs can echo those thoughts however I knew what I was doing, how long I would be there etc, but dogs don't, and it must be a bit of a stressful experience at first. It's the best feeling ever when one of those dogs finally relaxes under my touch and I can see the eyes gently starting to close, their limbs go heavy and they release a gentle sigh.

From: Helen Morphew 22 March 2016 at 15:00
To: Chicago School of Canine Massage
Subject: A little story for you...

Hey lovely,
How are you? Hope business is going well.
Do you remember when I was on the course that I said that I didn't want to work in the palliative care arena as I thought it would be too emotionally challenging for me? Hmmm, well here is a little story I wanted to share with you…
A local shelter recently appealed for volunteers to do extra shifts to help with the number of animals they had from a recent uplift.
Rather than give extra shifts as a volunteer, I was so moved by a video I saw showing the plight of two aged dogs that I was moved to offer my therapeutic services, free of charge. I wasn't sure if they would take me up on my offer when I made it, but thankfully they did. At the very start I knew full well that the animals I volunteered to work on

would not be able to be adopted out as their health conditions were extensive – cancer, arthritis, tumours, blind and / or deaf.

I have now spent four weeks, once a week, working on three dogs for 30 minutes each. The changes I noted in their behaviour from their first session with me, to their fourth session, which I had yesterday, has been really interesting. The one dog who was, to be honest, a bit of a pain in that first session, turned out to be the one most in need, and the one who stole my heart.

Yesterday was my final session with them – I don't need to tell you why – and were the hardest three sessions I have had to do. It took all my training and focus, and more importantly heart, to give them the care and work they needed so badly in their last sessions. I thanked each of them for letting me work on them as I took them back to their pens.

I can't help what happened to those gorgeous animals before they got to the shelter but working on them was so rewarding, to make their final twilight weeks happy, comfortable and full of love.

I went out for supper with a friend last night and suddenly burst into tears telling her about them. I guess I just hadn't realised how much it affected me. I feel so totally honoured to have had the chance to work on them and take the teachings they gave me.

I really really love what I do, despite the hard bits.

Just wanted to share that story with someone who would understand :)

Hxx

Musings

I t's been three years, 11 months since that hideous TV segment that I am delighted to say did not adversely affect my business. I have one client at least who I can directly attribute to the programme, and visiting their house is good for the soul.

They contacted me after watching the programme, understanding the merits of massage despite the efforts of the presenters to the contrary. I first visited them to work on their elderly dog Thai who was suffering from arthritis. They had another dog, Mack and a cat called Kevin. During each session I had with Thai, Mack would come and sit close by, keeping guard over his precious elder sister. At the end of each session I would distribute treats, not just to Thai but also to Mack. I don't have cat treats so I assumed that Kevin wouldn't want any, but oh no. Kevin thinks he too is a dog and would jump up onto the arm of the sofa and sit obediently waiting for his tasty morsel. As Thai was nearing the end of her life another dog, Frankie, joined the family. Sadly, Thai passed away and shortly after Mack became very sick. I didn't see them for a while, just popping round every so often on my way to or from nearby clients, to say hello and get my fix from the two dogs and the cat. Recently Mack's health has deteriorated, and they felt that a massage would be good for him. It was as if I'd never stopped treating them. All of us sitting around his soft bed on the floor in the living room while I worked on Mack, Frankie coming to sit close by and towards the end of the session so did Kevin – eagerly awaiting the treats he knew would follow.

Just the other day I was in a shop buying some clothes in between clients, as you do, and the girl looked at the logo on my t-shirt and exclaimed that it must be a dream job. For me it really is. I've worked hard but have enjoyed almost every minute of it. A magazine quoted recent estimates of New Zealand's companion animal population at 4.6 million – almost one for every human. Over the last few years I have noticed our views of the role of our dogs in our families evolving. People are more open to exploring complementary options, alongside conventional medical approaches. Dogs are living longer, one of my clients passed away recently at the grand old age of 18 years and nine months. And that doesn't seem that unusual any more. My desire to see canine massage develop into a mainstream offering is becoming a reality.

I have dipped in and out of my old human resources work over the last few years as well, nothing official. Mainly helping friends, supporting a charity with some recruitment and others with leadership coaching.

If you'd told me five years ago that I would be massaging dogs for a living, that I'd be on national TV, radio, in a national newspaper and in NEXT (a glossy magazine) I would have thought you'd lost your mind. Add to that, that I would then write a book about it because so many people told me how 'inspiring' they found my story. Seriously I would never have believed you. I have made my dream a reality, with a load of hard work, determination, supportive friends, and an incredible husband. I would like to thank everyone who has helped me on this voyage and with this book, some of your names have been changed – both dogs and humans – and some not. Without you all, this journey would not have been as enjoyable.

Since completing this book I found myself in the unenviable position of having a dog with a ruptured cranial cruciate ligament. I know this is relatively common, I've had enough clients over the years with the same issue, however I was unprepared for the depth of sadness that overwhelmed me when it happened to Asha.

She is now 12 days post TPLO (tibial plateau levelling osteotomy) surgery and is receiving daily massage from me, together with weekly rehabilitation from Steph and weekly – soon to be twice weekly – hydrotherapy. Managing her pain and comfort are my priority and I have found myself in the combined roles of massage therapist, client and owner.

Today she was allowed to be liberated from the 'Cone of Shame', the Elizabethan collar that she had to wear to prevent her licking at her incision, and us ending up in a whole new world of pain!

I have been making daily enrichment toys for her – a frozen Kong toy, a treat stuffed into an empty toilet roll holder, frozen silicone mats smeared with peanut butter or natural yogurt – anything that uses her brain energy rather than her physical energy to compensate for the restriction we have to endure for the next five-plus weeks.

To say I've been stressed is a little of an understatement. But we are progressing, and each day she is improving which is the most important thing.

Printed in Great Britain
by Amazon